新视界大学英语系列教材

Essential and Practical College English

基础实用英语听说教程

第三册 教师用书

总主编 马占祥
主　编 崔振华
副主编 林　涌
编　委 杨艳萍 刘　泉 李　慧 苏布德
　　　 王　倩 陈　焱 李晓英 胡啸翀

中国人民大学出版社
·北京·

新视界大学英语系列教材

《基础实用英语》
编委会

马占祥（内蒙古师范大学）

鲍　瑞（内蒙古师范大学）

巴达荣贵（内蒙古农业大学职业技术学院）

纪雪梅（内蒙古师范大学）

高桂贤（内蒙古兴安盟职业技术学院）

李文冀（锡林郭勒职业学院）

田振江（呼伦贝尔学院）

崔振华（内蒙古大学鄂尔多斯学院）

苏日嘎拉图（呼和浩特民族学院）

闫晓云（集宁师范学院）

前言

《基础实用英语》（*Essential and Practical College English*）是为少数民族地区高校学生编写的大学英语学习教材。 在教材的设计和编写上严格按照《大学英语课程教学要求》，并结合少数民族地区学生的实际英语水平，以打好英语基础和提高语言应用能力为最终目的，全力以赴，打造我国富有民族特色的新型大学英语教材。

本套教材在编写过程中，吸取了我国在外语教学中长期积累下来的行之有效的经验和方法，仔细研究和分析了我国少数民族学生在英语学习中经常遇到的问题及教师在教学过程中的困惑，在教材的编写理念和教学模式上不断创新，充分反映了当今外语教育研究的最新成果。

全套教材由《基础实用英语读写教程》（1～4 册）和《基础实用英语听说教程》（1～4 册）构成，每册设有八个单元，并配有详尽的教师用书和教学课件。教材内容以单元话题为主线，涉及现代技术、道德情感、文化知识、科学教育等多个方面。语言素材真实、地道，选材广泛，文章短小精悍，具有知识性、趣味性和实用性的鲜明特点。

本套教材起点为大学英语预备级和高职高专新生的入学水平。教学安排上，可分四个学期使用，也可以根据各学校的具体教学情况及学生的专业特点自行安排。教学总时数为 220 学时，每周安排3～4 学时。

本套教材由马占祥教授担任总主编，参加编写的院校有：内蒙古师范大学、内蒙古农业大学职业技术学院、内蒙古兴安盟职业技术学院、锡林郭勒职业学院、呼伦贝尔学院、内蒙古大学鄂尔多斯学院、呼和浩特民族学院和集宁师范学院。

各分册主编有鲍瑞、巴达荣贵、纪雪梅、高桂贤、李文冀、田振江、崔振华、苏日嘎拉图和闫晓云。初稿完成后，我们特地组织了一个由国内专家、学者以及教学经验丰富的一线老师组成的专家组对整套书稿进行了系统校阅。此外，在书稿的编写过程中，美籍教师 Amy Shane 对书稿进行了系统的审阅，并为我们提出了宝贵的意见和建议；中国人民大学出版社的领导和编辑对教材的编写工作给予了悉心指导和帮助，对他们的辛勤劳动，在此一并表示诚挚的谢意！

从整套教材的策划到最终定稿出版，我们始终坚持把好质量关，但在实际编写中难免还会出现纰漏和不妥之处，希望广大师生和专家学者在使用过程中不吝赐教，使之不断充实和完善！

有关本教材的教学课件，请联系 wyfsmail@163.com，或电话：010-62512737，010-62515576，010-62513265，010-62515037。

编委会

2012年12月

于呼和浩特

Contents

Traveling

Aims

- Making a Reservation
- Talking About a Tourist Site

 **Warm-up**

 Fill in the blanks with the following words or phrases.

| purchase | train | travel | passport | boarding passes |
| flight | customs | arrangement | boarding gate | inquire |

1. Do you like to _____ on holiday?

2. You can choose to travel by _____.

3. We need to _____ a ticket before we plan to travel to some places.

4. The next _____ from Shanghai Pudong International Airport is scheduled to arrive at 3:15 p.m.

5. If you want to travel abroad, you have to get a _____ in advance.

6. It is necessary to make a/an _____ to make your trip perfect.

7. You have to check in at the _____ .

8. Please form in line and have your _____ ready for second inspection.

9. You can _____ the tourist information center to deal with some problems about traveling.

10. Do you have any idea about how long it will take to clear _____?

Now listen and check.

LANGUAGE TIPS

purchase: 购买	schedule: 安排	clear customs: 通关
boarding gate: 登机口	inspection: 检验，检查	passport: 护照
tourism information center: 旅游咨询中心	reservation: 预订	check in: 登记

TEACHING TIP

Ask students to fill the missing words in the statements and then listen to the recordings to check the answers.

I. Warm-up

 Scripts:

1. Do you like to <u>travel</u> on holiday?

2. You can choose to travel by <u>train</u>.

3. We need to <u>purchase</u> a ticket before we plan to travel to some places.

4. The next <u>flight</u> from Shanghai Pudong International Airport is scheduled to arrive at 3:15 p.m.

5. If you want to travel abroad, you have to get a <u>passport</u> in advance.

6. It is necessary to make a/an <u>arrangement</u> to make your trip perfect.

7. You have to check in at the <u>boarding gate</u>.

8. Please form in line and have your <u>boarding passes</u> ready for second inspection.

9. You can <u>inquire</u> the tourist information center to deal with some problems about traveling.

10. Do you have any idea about how long it will take to clean <u>customs</u>?

II Listening Focus: Making a Hotel Reservation

🎧 Listen to the dialogue and fill in the blanks.

A: I would like to book a reservation at your hotel.

B: What date would you like to make that reservation for?

A: I need the reservation for _____ .

B: How many days do you need the reservation for?

A: I will be staying for _____ .

B: Is that a _____ , or will there be more guests?

A: I need a _____ .

B: We have smoking and _____ rooms. Which do you prefer?

A: We require a smoking room.

B: Your room is booked. You must arrive before _____ the day you are to check in.

II. Listening Focus: Making a Hotel Reservation

 Script:

A: I would like to book a reservation at your hotel.

B: What date would you like to make that reservation for?

A: I need the reservation for May 14th.

B: How many days do you need the reservation for?

A: I will be staying for three nights.

B: Is that a single room, or will there be more guests?

A: I need a double room.

B: We have smoking and non-smoking rooms. Which do you prefer?

A: We require a smoking room.

B: Your room is booked. You must arrive before 4:00 the day you are to check in.

Listening Practice

Task 1

Listen to the following passage, and choose the best answer to each of the questions.

1. According to the Ministry of Railways, how long will the Spring Festival travel season last?

   A. 11 days.

   B. 25 days.

   C. 40 days.

   D. 45 days.

2. When is the Lantern Festival?

   A. January 11th.

   B. February 25th.

   C. January 26th.

   D. February 9th.

LANGUAGE AND CULTURE TIPS

Spring Festival travel rush: 春运高峰

passenger flow: 客流　　　semester: 学期

3. In 2009, the number of average passenger flow is _____ every day.

   A. 188 million

   B. 47 million

   C. 4.7 million

   D. 340 million

4. Which flow of people who have made the passenger peak come early is NOT mentioned in the passage?

   A. College students.

   B. Businessmen.

   C. Migrant workers.

   D. Travelers.

5. What measure does the railway department take to deal with the travel rush?

   A. Put into use of additional passenger trains.

   B. Prepare three operating schemes.

   C. Reschedule the time.

   D. Advise colleges to begin their semester later.

III. Listening Practice

Task 1

> **TEACHING TIP**
>
> Play the passage three times, and then ask the students to try to get the main idea of the whole passage and encourage them to answer the questions.

 Keys:

1. C   2. D   3. C   4. B   5. A

 Script:

Spring Festival Travel Rush to Start on January 11th

The Chinese Ministry of Railways says the 2009 Spring Festival travel season will be from January 11th to February 25th.

Wang Yongping, spokesman of the ministry, said on Monday that the 40-day travel season will span the Chinese Lunar New Year, which falls on January 26th, and the Lantern Festival on February 9th.

He said the overall passenger flow is expected to hit 188 million, up 8% year on year. And the average passenger flow is expected to be 4.7 million every day, 340,000 more than the same period in 2008.

During the Spring Festival travel season of 2009, flows of college students, migrant workers and travelers will overlap before the Lunar New Year, making the passenger peak come early. After the Spring Festival, migrant workers may travel back a little bit earlier. But the whole situation of passenger flow is still unclear, given that college students may travel back in the end of the travel season because the new semester begins later.

During the travel rush, the railway department will put into use 319 pairs of additional nonstop passenger trains. It has also prepared three operating schemes to deal with regular, peak and sudden passenger flows.

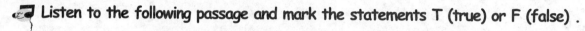

Task 2

🔊 Listen to the following passage and mark the statements T (true) or F (false).

_____ 1. People enjoy taking trips because they want to broaden their horizons and learn about other people and other places.

_____ 2. Tourists are not very interested in other kinds of life style.

_____ 3. Visiting museums and historical spots can help people learn about local culture.

_____ 4. There is more than 200 square meters of space for each person in Hong Kong.

_____ 5. Hong Kong has the moving lines of tall modern buildings.

🔊 Now listen and check.

LANGUAGE TIPS

broaden one's horizons: 开阔视野   scenic spot: 风景名胜区

vehicle: 车辆   vertical: 垂直的

Task 2

 Keys:

1. T   2. F   3. T   4. F   5. F

 Script:

People enjoy taking trips because they want to broaden their horizons, learn about other people and other places.

Generally speaking, they are very curious about other cultures. When traveling, they get a quick look at different ways of living.

On a trip, a person can learn directly by visiting museums and historical spots. When a tourist visits the historical palaces and other scenic spots in Paris, he gets a vivid picture—a real life of the French people. He learns about their attitudes, how they feel about business, beauty and history.

What about the tourist who goes to Hong Kong? He might read about the fact from a book that Hong Kong is very crowded, and that there is less than 200 square meters of space for each person, but seeing and feeling the lack of space will impress him much more. He might read about the fact that there are nearly 200 vehicles for every kilometer of roadway, but the sight of so many vehicles parked along the roadside will be a much more vivid lesson. The tourist to Hong Kong will never forget the contrasts—the straight vertical lines of tall modern buildings and the moving lines of boats that people live in.

Task 3: Listen for Fun

 Listen to the song and fill in the blanks with the missing words.

> ### LANGUAGE AND CULTURE TIPS
>
> falter: 支吾（地说）；蹒跚地走
> drift: 漂流，漂移，漂泊
> Calvary:【圣经】骷髅地（耶稣被钉死在十字架上的地方，见《路加福音》）
> Satan: 撒旦，《圣经》中的恶魔（或称魔鬼撒旦），反叛耶和华的堕落天使（Fallen Angel）。他曾经是上帝座前的六翼天使，负责在人间放置诱惑。后来他堕落成为魔鬼，被看做是与光明力量相对的邪恶、黑暗之源。
> foes:（ foe 的复数形式）敌人，反对者
>
> block: 阻止，限制
> by one's side: 在身旁

Journey

It's a long long journey
Till I know where I'm _____ to be
It's a long long journey
I don't know if I can _____
When shadows fall and block my eyes
I am lost and know that I must _____
It's a long long journey
Till I find my way home to you
Many days I've _____
Drifting on through empty shores
_____ what's my purpose
Wondering how to make me strong
I know I will falter I know I will _____
I know you'll be standing by my side
It's a long long journey
And I need to be close to you
Sometimes it feels no one _____
I don't even know why I do the things I do
When pride builds me up till I can't see my soul
Will you break down these walls and _____ me through
Because it's a long long journey
Till I feel that I am _____ the price
You paid for me on calvary
_____ those stormy skies
When Satan mocks and friends turn to foes
It feels like everything is out to make me lose control
Because it's a long long journey
Till I find my way home to you...to you

Task 3: Listen for fun

 Script:

Journey

It's a long long journey

Till I know where I'm <u>supposed</u> to be

It's a long long journey

I don't know if I can <u>believe</u>

When shadows fall and block my eyes

I am lost and know that I must <u>hide</u>

It's a long long journey

Till I find my way home to you

Many days I've <u>spent</u>

Drifting on through empty shores

<u>Wondering</u> what's my purpose

Wondering how to make me strong

I know I will falter I know I will <u>cry</u>

I know you'll be standing by my side

It's a long long journey

And I need to be close to you

Sometimes it feels no one <u>understands</u>

I don't even know why I do the things I do

When pride builds me up till I can't see my soul

Will you break down these walls and <u>pull</u> me through

Because it's a long long journey

Till I feel that I am <u>worth</u> the price

You paid for me on calvary

<u>Beneath</u> those stormy skies

When Satan mocks and friends turn to foes

It feels like everything is out to make me lose control

Because it's a long long journey

Till I find my way home to you…to you

IV Look and Talk

 Look at the pictures. Please match the pictures with the names given in the following table.

Picture 1 _____

Picture 2 _____

Picture 3 _____

Picture 4 _____

Picture 5 _____

Picture 6 _____

The Potala Palace	The Pyramids
The Leaning Tower of Pisa	The Statue of Liberty
The Forbidden City	The Summer Palace

Model:

Lily: Isn't the palace museum called "the Forbidden City"?

Tom: Yes, it was. The Forbidden City is the imperial palace for the Ming and Qing Dynasties. Now it is referred to as the "Palace Museum."

Lily: From the looks of this picture, it seems like the Forbidden City, which is well-preserved.

Tom: With more than 500 years of history, it is the largest and most well-preserved imperial residence in China.

Lily: The Forbidden City must be the most famous cultural relic in China, huh?

Tom: Yeah, it was also recognized as a world cultural legacy by UNESCO in 1988.

LANGUAGE AND CULTURE TIPS

the Forbidden City: 紫禁城（现为故宫博物院）
imperial: 帝国的；皇帝的；至高无上的；威严的
dynasty: 王朝，朝代
well-preserved: 保存良好的
UNESCO: *abbr.* 联合国教科文组织（United Nations Educational, Scientific, and Cultural Organization）

Now Your Turn:

1. Work in pairs to make similar dialogues about other pictures.

2. Try to use other sentences and expressions listed below.

Useful Sentences and Expressions:

Would you please tell me something about…?
Could you give me some information about…, Mr./Mrs./Miss…?
It is world-famous especially for its…
…bring together the beauties of nature, architecture and painting.
I'd like to take a one-day sightseeing tour around…
Shall we take a tour to…, Mr./Mrs./Miss…?
…is the largest and the best preserved of…in…
It covers an area of…hectares.

IV. Look and Talk

TEACHING TIP

1. Tell the class to look at the pictures, and then ask several students to report the main information in the pictures.
2. To model how to use the clues, you may ask one of the students to be your partner and act out the dialogues.
3. For the part "Now Your Turn," divide the class into pairs to prepare the dialogues. Walk around the class and give help as needed.
4. The students should feel free to talk about any of the six pictures and they can add some information according to the useful sentences and expressions.

 Keys:

Picture 1   The Summer Palace
Picture 2   The Potala Palace
Picture 3   The Forbidden City
Picture 4   The Leaning Tower of Pisa
Picture 5   The Pyramids
Picture 6   The Statue of Liberty

 Sample:

Lily: The Summer Palace is one of the most famous imperial gardens. During various periods of war, it suffered extensive damages.

Tom: It's a surprise that the Summer Palace is so well-preserved.

Lily: It was rebuilt about one hundred years ago and has been through many processes of restoration.

Tom: Is that hill in the distance a part of the Summer Palace?

Lily: No, that hill is called Yuquan Hill and isn't a part of the Summer Palace. The only hill that is a part of the Summer Palace is Wanshou Hill.

Tom: What an ingenious layout! It completely incorporates its natural surroundings.

Lily: Let's set off right away.

Tom: Let's go!

Love and Marriage

Aims

- Listening for the Information About Wedding
- Talking About Difference

I Warm-up

Fill in the blanks with the following words.

wedding	honeymoon	attend	gown	event	traditionally
engagement	popular	groom	toast		

1. _____ , the bride's parents pay for the wedding.

2. The most _____ months of wedding are June, July and August.

3. Keith bought his girlfriend a beautiful _____ ring at a high price.

4. The wedding included traditions from both religions of the bride and the _____ .

5. The bride and the groom _____ each other and the guests cheer.

6. The wedding planner helps the bride find a _____ dress as well as dresses for her bridesmaids.

7. The bride may buy a used _____ rather than pay thousands of dollars for a new one.

8. Tom and his wife will be ready to leave for their _____ .

9. About four hundred people reportedly _____ the wedding.

10. Guests were not told where the wedding was to be held until a week before the _____ .

Now listen and check.

LANGUAGE TIPS

engagement: 订婚；婚约
gown: 女礼服

> **TEACHING TIP**
>
> Ask students to fill in the blanks in the sentences and then listen to the recordings to check their answers.

I. Warm-up

 Scripts:

1. <u>Traditionally</u>, the bride's parents pay for the wedding.

2. The most <u>popular</u> months of wedding are June, July and August.

3. Keith bought his girlfriend a beautiful <u>engagement</u> ring at a high price.

4. The wedding included traditions from both religions of the bride and the <u>groom</u>.

5. The bride and the groom <u>toast</u> each other and the guests cheer.

6. The wedding planner helps the bride find a <u>wedding</u> dress as well as dresses for her bridesmaids.

7. The bride may buy a used <u>gown</u> rather than pay thousands of dollars for a new one.

8. Tom and his wife will be ready to leave for their <u>honeymoon</u>.

9. About four hundred people reportedly <u>attend</u> the wedding.

10. Guests were not told where the wedding was to be held until a week before the <u>event</u>.

II Listening Focus

Listen to the following dialogues and match the topics with them.

_____ Dialogue 1   A. Wedding Anniversary

_____ Dialogue 2   B. Vowing in Church

_____ Dialogue 3   C. Wedding Ceremony

_____ Dialogue 4   D. Making a Proposal

_____ Dialogue 5   E. Dating

LANGUAGE TIPS

tie the knot: 结婚

bouquet: 花束

II. Listening Focus

D	Dialogue 1	A. Wedding Anniversary
A	Dialogue 2	B. Vowing in Church
B	Dialogue 3	C. Wedding Ceremony
E	Dialogue 4	D. Making a Proposal
C	Dialogue 5	E. Dating

 Scripts:

Dialogue 1:

M: Mary, I have something for you and it is very special.

W: Special?

M: Definitely.

W: Wow, a ring! Beautiful!

M: Mary, this is an important question that I've never asked before. Will you marry me?

W: Oh…Yes, I will.

M: I plan to hold the wedding next June. Is that all right?

W: That's perfect.

Dialogue 2:

M: I don't know if you remember, but it was on this day last year that we tied the knot.

W: Of course I remember. Actually, I'm very impressed that you remembered. I thought for sure you would forget.

M: How could I ever forget? I even bought you roses because I love you.

W: They are so beautiful. I love them and I love you too.

M: You are more beautiful than the roses.

W: I don't know why, but I love you more now than the day we got married.

M: Yes, we are a match made in heaven.

W: I know over the past year we have faced our share of trouble, but we survived and here we are.

M: Yes, indeed, we did have problems, but we share a lot of happiness too. We conquered the problems and had a lot of happiness too.

W: Yes, we did.

M: I love you! Happy anniversary!

W: I love you! Happy anniversary!

Dialogue 3:

Officiator: Jack, do you take Mary to be your lawfully wedded wife?

M: I do.

Officiator: Mary, do you take Jack to be your lawfully wedded husband?

W: I do.

M &W: For better, for worse, for richer, for poorer, in sickness and in health, till death do we part.

Officiator: The rings, please. I now pronounce you a husband and wife. May your marriage bring you great happiness.

Dialogue 4:

W: I'm sorry, something's come up. Can we make our appointment tomorrow?

M: Yes.

W: That'll be fine. I'm terribly sorry to bring you inconvenience.

M: That's all right. I don't mind at all.

Dialogue 5:

M: Hi, Lucy!

W: Hi. It's a wonderful wedding, isn't it?

M: Yes. It's great.

W: Mary's father is a rich man, isn't he?

M: You are right. Mary's father is responsible for the entire wedding arrangement, costs, etc. I think he must have spent much money.

W: Will Mary and her husband be ready to leave for their honeymoon?

M: Yes. Look! Mary is going to throw the bride bouquet.

W: Oh, I'll try to catch it.

 Listening Practice

Task 1

🎧 Listen to the dialogue and choose the best answer for each question.

1. What is the probable relationship between the two speakers?

   A. Husband and wife.　　　　　B. Good friends.

   C. Boss and clerk.　　　　　　D. Teacher and student.

2. How do you understand the sentence in the dialogue "Someone has a crush on Sarah"?

   A. Someone uses severe methods to stop Sarah from fighting him.

   B. Someone makes Sarah feel extremely upset.

   C. Someone has an uncontrollable feeling of love for Sarah.

   D. Someone makes Sarah lose all hope.

3. Which word can replace the phrase "turn down" in the dialogue?

   A. Accept.　　　　　　　　　B. Substitute.

   C. Refuse.　　　　　　　　　D. Offer.

> **LANGUAGE TIPS**
>
> flame red:（脸）涨红
> chicken: 胆小的人
> guts: 勇气

4. What is Gilbert afraid of?

   A. He is afraid of being made a fool of.　　B. He is afraid of being refused.

   C. He is afraid of being asked.　　　　　　D. He is afraid of being hit.

5. What does Henry suggest to Gilbert?

   A. He should tell Sarah his true feeling.　　B. He should keep his secret.

   C. He should only wait.　　　　　　　　　D. He should do nothing.

Ⅲ. Listening Practice

Task 1

> **TEACHING TIP**
>
> Play this dialogue three times, and then ask the students to retell the story according to what they hear. Walk around the classroom and give help as needed.

 Script:

M: Hey, Nancy, is Sarah coming with us?

W: Yes. Why?

M: Nothing. I'm just asking.

W: Just asking? But why is your face flaming red? Ah-huh, someone has a crush on Sarah, doesn't he?

M: Who has a crush?!

W: Come on, Gilbert, don't be such a chicken. If you like her, just go and tell her. Maybe she likes you.

M: But I don't have the guts to ask her out.

W: What are you so afraid of?

M: I'd totally die if she turned me down.

W: But that's better than keeping everything to yourself. You've got to let her know. Come on! You've got to take a chance!

M: I don't know… Well, maybe you're right, but how am I going to tell her I like her?

 Keys:

1. B   2. C   3. C   4. B   5. A

Task 2

 Listen to the passage and fill in the blanks with the missing words.

Each year, more than two million weddings take place in the United States. The most popular months are June, July and August. More than seventy billion dollars is spent on those weddings. And that does not _____ honeymoon travel for the _____ . Some people have a big wedding and invite everyone they know. Some have a small, simple wedding and invite only their _____ friends and family members. And some elope. They get married first and tell people later. Some couples have a _____ ceremony. Others have a civil wedding before a judge or some other _____ . And some have both. During a wedding, the couple might read special _____ or promises that they have written for each other. Many ceremonies share common customs. For example, the bride may wear a long white dress and have a white _____ over her face. And old tradition says brides should wear something old, something new, something borrowed and something blue. These four things are _____ to bring good luck. The groom _____ wears a tuxedo. Picture a nervous penguin if the suit is black and the shirt is white. Usually the bride's father or another _____ walks her down the aisle and presents her to the groom. Sometimes both parents share this tradition.

LANGUAGE TIPS

big wedding: 盛大的婚礼　　elope: 私奔

civil wedding: 民间婚礼　　tuxedo: 男士无尾礼服

penguin: 企鹅

walk sb. down the aisle: 领着某人走过红地毯

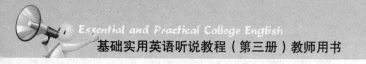
Task 2

 Script:

Each year, more than two million weddings take place in the United States. The most popular months are June, July and August. More than seventy billion dollars is spent on those weddings. And that does not <u>include</u> honeymoon travel for the <u>newlyweds</u>. Some people have a big wedding and invite everyone they know. Some have a small, simple wedding and invite only their <u>closest</u> friends and family members. And some elope. They get married first and tell people later. Some couples have a <u>religious</u> ceremony. Others have a civil wedding before a judge or some other <u>official</u>. And some have both. During a wedding, the couple might read special <u>vows</u> or promises that they have written for each other. Many ceremonies share common customs. For example, the bride may wear a long white dress and have a white <u>veil</u> over her face. And old tradition says brides should wear something old, something new, something borrowed and something blue. These four things are <u>supposed</u> to bring good luck. The groom <u>traditionally</u> wears a tuxedo. Picture a nervous penguin if the suit is black and the shirt is white. Usually the bride's father or another <u>relative</u> walks her down the aisle and presents her to the groom. Sometimes both parents share this tradition.

Task 3: Listen for Fun

🎵 Listen to the song and fill in the blanks with the missing words.

My Heart Will Go On

Every night in my _____
I see you, I _____ you
That is _____ I know you go on
Far across the _____ and_____ between us
You have come to _____ you go on
Near, far, _____ you are
I _____ that the heart does go on
Once more you _____ the door
And you're _____ in my heart
And my heart will go on and on

Love can touch us one time
And last for a lifetime
And never let go till we're gone
Love was when I loved you
One true time I hold to
In my life we'll always go on
Near far wherever you are
I believe that the heart does go on
Once more you open the door
And you're here in my heart
And my heart will go on and on

You're here
There's nothing I fear
And I know that my heart will go on
We'll stay forever this way
You are safe in my heart
And my heart will go on and on

Task 3: Listen for Fun

 *Script:*

My Heart Will Go On

Every night in my dreams

I see you, I feel you

That is how I know you go on

Far across the distance and spaces between us

You have come to show you go on

Near, far, wherever you are

I believe that the heart does go on

Once more you opened the door

And you're here in my heart

And my heart will go on and on

Love can touch us one time

And last for a lifetime

And never let go till we're gone

Love was when I loved you

One true time I hold to

In my life we'll always go on

Near far wherever you are

I believe that the heart does go on

Once more you open the door

And you're here in my heart

And my heart will go on and on

You're here

There's nothing I fear

And I know that my heart will go on

We'll stay forever this way

You are safe in my heart

And my heart will go on and on

Ⅳ Look and Talk

Look at the following table. It shows the differences between Chinese wedding and Western wedding.

Chinese Wedding			Western Wedding		
Color	Red		Color	Black and White	
Clothes	Bride	Cheongsam	Clothes	Bride	Wedding Garment
	Groom	Suit		Groom	Tuxedo
Place	Restaurant		Place	Church	
Host	Master of Ceremonies		Host	Pastor	

Susan and Mike are talking about the differences between Chinese wedding and Western wedding.

Model:

S: What do you think of the differences between Chinese wedding and Western wedding?

M: It varies a lot.

S: Would you please give us some examples for that?

M: Sure. For instance, red is the color appeared most in Chinese wedding, as it represents good luck and indicates that couples will live happily ever after. However, black and white are most commonly used in Western wedding, as they represent the sublimity of marriage.

S: Yes, that is obvious.

M: There are also differences in what people wear in their wedding. In China, brides wear Chinese traditional cheongsam, while in the West brides usually wear white wedding garment.

S: Thank you for sharing that with me.

Now Your Turn:

1. Work in pairs and try to talk about the differences between Chinese wedding and Western wedding using the content in the table above.

2. Try to use other expressions listed below and talk about the differences between Chinese wedding and Western wedding.

Useful Sentences and Expressions:

Could you say something about the differences between…and…?

Can you tell me the most different part in…?

The differences between Chinese wedding and Western wedding are that…

…would like to hold the wedding in church, while…prefer to have it in restaurant.

…like a church wedding, but…like a civil ceremony.

IV. Look and Talk

 Sample:

S: Could you say something about the differences between Chinese wedding and Western wedding?

M: It varies a lot.

S: Would you please give us some examples for that?

M: Sure. For instance, in Chinese wedding the bride always wears a cheongsam and the groom wears a suit, as they represent good luck and indicate that couples will live happily ever after. However, in Western wedding the bride wears a wedding garment and the groom wears a tuxedo, as they represent the sublimity of marriage.

S: Yes, that is obvious.

M: There are also differences in where the wedding ceremony holds. In China, it is held in a restaurant while in the West it is usually held in church.

S: Thank you for sharing that with me.

Chinese and Americans

Aims

- Listening for Cultural Difference
- Talking About Table Etiquettes

I Warm-up

Fill in the blanks with the following words or phrases.

| follow suit | in low spirit | contribute to | adapt | customs |
| culture shock | newcomer | differently | weird | proverb |

> **LANGUAGE TIPS**
>
> follow suit: 跟着做，照着做
> culture shock: 文化冲击
> in low spirit: 情绪低落
> weird: 古怪的，离奇的

1. As a _____ I don't know how to get along well with the local people.

2. You have to _____ yourself to the life in America.

3. The values I hold and the way I lead my life become totally _____ in this country.

4. I have been _____ since I came to China.

5. Have you heard the _____ "When in Rome, do as the Romans do"?

6. Different places have different cultures and _____ , and the safest way is always to mimic the locals.

7. You might be considered as weird if you don't _____ in a new culture.

8. Most people experience some degree of _____ when they go to a new country.

9. Many factors can _____ culture shock—smell, sound, flavor, and the feeling of the air one is breathing.

10. We Chinese think _____ from Americans.

Now listen and check.

I. Warm-up

 Scripts:

1. As a <u>newcomer</u> I don't know how to get along well with the local people.

2. You have to <u>adapt</u> yourself to the life in America.

3. The values I hold and the way I lead my life become totally <u>weird</u> in this country.

4. I have been <u>in low spirit</u> since I came to China.

5. Have you heard the <u>proverb</u> "When in Rome, do as the Romans do"?

6. Different places have different cultures and <u>customs</u>, and the safest way is always to mimic the locals.

7. You might be considered as weird if you don't <u>follow suit</u> in a new culture.

8. Most people experience some degree of <u>culture shock</u> when they go to a new country.

9. Many factors can <u>contribute to</u> culture shock—smell, sound, flavor, and the feeling of the air one is breathing.

10. We Chinese think <u>differently</u> from Americans.

II Listening Focus

Listen for the numbers offering general information about China and the USA.

1. The United States of America is a federal constitutional republic comprising _____ states and a federal district.

2. China has jurisdiction over _____ provinces, _____ autonomous regions _____ direct-controlled municipalities and _____ special administrative regions.

3. At _____ square miles (9.83 million km²) and with over _____ people, the United States is the _____ largest country by total area, and the _____ largest by population.

4. China is the world's most populous country, with a population of over _____ . This East Asian state covers a territory of approximately _____ square kilometers of land and nearly _____ square kilometers of ocean and sea, and is the world's third largest in total area.

5. China's coastline along the Pacific Ocean is _____ kilometers long, and is bounded by the Bohai, Yellow, East and South China Seas.

TEACHING TIP

Play this part twice, and then ask the students to talk about the differences between China and the USA.

Ⅱ. Listening Focus

 Scripts:

1. The United States of America is a federal constitutional republic comprising <u>fifty</u> states and a federal district.

2. China has jurisdiction over <u>23</u> provinces, <u>five</u> autonomous regions, <u>four</u> direct-controlled municipalities and <u>two</u> special administrative regions.

3. At <u>3.79 million</u> square miles (9.83 million km²) and with over <u>312 million</u> people, the United States is the <u>fourth</u> largest country by total area, and the <u>third</u> largest by population.

4. China is the world's most populous country, with a population of over <u>1.3 billion</u>. This East Asian state covers a territory of approximately <u>9.6 million</u> square kilometers of land and nearly <u>3 million</u> square kilometers of ocean and sea, and is the world's third largest in total area.

5. China's coastline along the Pacific Ocean is <u>18,000</u> kilometers long, and is bounded by the Bohai, Yellow, East and South China Seas.

III Listening Practice

Task 1

 Listen to the speakers' evaluations on their experiences in the USA or China, and choose the best answer to each of the questions.

LANGUAGE TIPS

embarrass: 使……尴尬
hospitable: 热情的
appetite: 食欲，胃口

1. What made Shen Fang feel that she was not really welcome?

   A. She stayed for the whole evening, and was about to leave.

   B. She was an unexpected visitor.

   C. Her friend went back to his room closing the door behind him as soon as they said goodbye.

   D. She adjusted well to the American way of life soon after arriving in the USA.

2. Why did the other Americans stare at Dai Qi and Janice?

   A. They ordered too much food in the restaurant.   B. They ate as if there were no tomorrow.

   C. Dai Qi talked too loud in the restaurant.   D. Janice talked too loud in the restaurant.

3. What was one of George's special experiences in China?

   A. He was invited to a Chinese family for dinner.

   B. He had a good appetite and ate a lot of delicious food.

   C. He got more food by asking for more.

   D. His host kept on putting more food in his rice bowl even when he said, "No, thank you."

4. What was amazing for Annie?

   A. Americans are extremely hospitable.

   B. Her friend's grandfather insisted on walking her to the station to see her off though she knew the way.

   C. Her friend's grandfather walked to the station all by himself.

   D. She found her friend's grandfather stayed at home all by himself.

5. Which of the following is true according to George and Annie's experiences?

   A. American people don't understand the speaker's Chinese way of talking.

   B. Chinese people don't understand the speaker's American way of talking.

   C. Chinese ask for more delicious food during the dinner if they really want.

   D. Americans don't ask for more delicious food during the dinner if they really want.

 **Now listen and check.**

III. Listening Practice

Task 1

 Keys:

1. C   2. C   3. D   4. B   5. B

> **TEACHING TIP**
>
> Play this part three times, and then remind the students of paying attention to the culture shock.

 Scripts:

(Shen Fang and Dai Qi are two Chinese overseas students in the USA and the following are their experiences and feelings in the foreign country.)

Shen Fang: When I first arrived in San Francisco, I had a difficult time understanding the American way of doing things. Once I went to visit an American friend. After staying for the whole evening, I was about to leave. But as soon as we said goodbye, my friend went back to his room closing the door behind him. It made me feel that I was not really welcome.

Dai Qi: I once had an embarrassing experience in a New York restaurant. I was talking to my American friend Janice at the table when I noticed people staring at us. I asked Janice what was wrong and she told me that I was talking too loud. She said to some American people my sound was like shouting.

(George and Annie are sharing their stories in China.)

George: What did I learn from my exciting cultural exchange to China? Well, the Chinese are extremely hospitable. One evening, I was invited to a Chinese family for dinner. I had a good appetite and ate a lot of delicious food. My host kept on putting more food in my rice bowl. They didn't seem to hear me saying, "No, thank you." This was a special experience I had in China. In my culture, you don't get more food if you don't ask for more.

Annie: I had a similar experience last time when I visited China. The Chinese are the most friendly people I have ever met. After my visit to a Chinese family, my friend's grandfather insisted on walking me to the station to see me off. I kept saying that I knew the way, but it just didn't work. What he did was amazing. This will not happen in other cultures, I guess.

Task 2

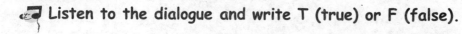

Listen to the dialogue and write T (true) or F (false).

_____ 1. Wen Hui is unhappy about her life in the United States.

_____ 2. Wen Hui likes the American way of doing things.

_____ 3. She understands that the majority of Americans believe in God.

_____ 4. Steven suggests Wen Hui visit a local family to get herself accustomed to the local culture.

_____ 5. Wen Hui wants to go to Rome.

Now listen and check.

> **LANGUAGE TIPS**
>
> lovesick: 害相思病的
> homesick: 想家的，思乡的
> conservative: 守旧的，保守的

Task 2

Keys:

1. T   2. F   3. T   4. F   5. F

> ### TEACHING TIP
>
> Play this dialogue three times, and then ask the students to retell the story according to what they hear.

Script:

Wen Hui: I am feeling a bit like a fish out of water. I have been in low spirit since I came to the States.

Steven: Lovesick or homesick, Wen Hui?

Wen Hui: Homesick, of course. Every night I dream of my family and I have a lot of problems here. I don't want to show up in public places and I don't like the way people do things.

Steven: For example?

Wen Hui: For example, you hug and kiss people so often. It's distinguishing. I'm conservative and I don't think it's right.

Steven: You have to adapt to it. It's our culture in which you are living. Have you ever heard the proverb "When in Rome, do as the Romans do"?

Wen Hui: You know, when I see local people, I think I belong to another species. We are so different. You are so white and tall and the majority believe in God. You have some strange traditions.

Steven: Don't be so serious about all this. Everything will be okay. You'll soon be accustomed to this culture, then you'll feel comfortable about living here.

Wen Hui: I hope so.

Steven: But you should be bold and not limit yourself within the circle of your countrymen. Get to know the local people. They are hospitable and will give you the warmest welcome.

Task 3: Listen for Fun

Listen to an American talking about his experience in China, and then fill in the blanks with the missing words.

LANGUAGE TIPS

obsess: 使着迷
banquet:（正式的）宴会，盛会
fabulous: 令人震惊的
hoof: 蹄
stinky: 恶臭的
choudoufu: 臭豆腐

Chinese people think a lot about food. In fact, I think that they are sometimes obsessed with it. My first experience of this aspect of Chinese culture came at a banquet during a trip to Beijing in 1998. I had eaten Chinese food often, but I could not have imagined how fabulous a real Chinese banquet could be. The first six or seven _____ seemed to fill the table. I thought this vast wave of food was the total _____ of dishes to be served, and I started eating greedily. Everyone else just tasted a bit of each dish and then put their _____ down, continuing to chat. "They can't have very big appetites," I thought.

To my surprise, more dishes arrived, plus soups, side dishes and desserts. There was enough to feed _____ . No wonder my fellow guests had only a few bits of each dish; they knew what was still to come. But I was already so full that I could only watch as _____ .

Another aspect of "food culture" is that the Chinese seem to eat almost _____ every animal— much to the horror of many Westerners. Stomach, ears, tongue, tail, hoof and lungs are all likely to end up on the dinner table _____ you.

These days I enjoy that sort of food myself. However, there are other kinds of foods that have _____ me to accept. The infamous *choudoufu* is an example. (The name says it all: "stinky tofu.") Just when _____ , I found another variety on a trip to Hunan: deep-fried *choudoufu*, a horrible _____ that looked and smelled about as appetizing as a burnt tennis shoe. Maybe I'll get used to that, too—someday.

Now listen and check.

Task 3: Listen for Fun

 Script:

Chinese people think a lot about food. In fact, I think that they are sometimes obsessed with it. My first experience of this aspect of Chinese culture came at a banquet during a trip to Beijing in 1998. I had eaten Chinese food often, but I could not have imagined how fabulous a real Chinese banquet could be. The first six or seven <u>dishes</u> seemed to fill the table. I thought this vast wave of food was the total <u>number</u> of dishes to be served, and I started eating greedily. Everyone else just tasted a bit of each dish and then put their <u>chopsticks</u> down, continuing to chat. "They can't have very big appetites," I thought.

To my surprise, more dishes arrived, plus soups, side dishes and desserts. There was enough to feed <u>a whole army</u>. No wonder my fellow guests had only a few bits of each dish; they knew what was still to come. But I was already so full that I could only watch as <u>the banquet continued</u>.

Another aspect of "food culture" is that the Chinese seem to eat almost <u>every part of</u> every animal— much to the horror of many Westerners. Stomach, ears, tongue, tail, hoof and lungs are all likely to end up on the dinner table <u>in front of</u> you.

These days I enjoy that sort of food myself. However, there are other kinds of foods that have <u>taken longer for</u> me to accept. The infamous *choudoufu* is an example. (The name says it all: "stinky tofu.") Just when <u>I got used to it</u>, I found another variety on a trip to Hunan: deep-fried *choudoufu*, a horrible <u>black substance</u> that looked and smelled about as appetizing as a burnt tennis shoe. Maybe I'll get used to that, too—someday.

IV Listen and Talk

You are going to hear some suggestions on good table etiquette in the USA.

Now Your Turn:

Please talk about good table etiquette in China.

Tips:

1. Who begins drinking or eating?

2. If you want to serve yourself with some food or tea, what should you do?

3. Can you pass the food around at the table?

4. Is it proper to take the last piece of food?

5. How to use chopsticks?

6. How to toast?

LANGUAGE TIPS

etiquette: 礼仪

clockwise: 顺时针方向

chopsticks: 筷子

IV. Listen and Talk

TEACHING TIP

Before listening, ask the students what good table manners are and what we should do to keep good table manners.

 Script:

Dinner Table Etiquette — The 10 Do's in the USA

1. Once seated, unfold your napkin and use it for occasionally wiping your lips or fingers. At the end of the dinner, leave the napkin tidily on the place setting.

2. It is good dinner table etiquette to serve the lady sitting to the right of the host first, then the other ladies in a clockwise direction, and lastly the gentlemen.

3. Hold the knife and fork with the handles in the palm of the hand, forefinger on top, and thumb underneath.

4. Whilst eating, you may if you wish rest the knife and fork on either side of the plate between mouthfuls. When you have finished eating, place them side by side in the center of the plate.

5. If the food presented to you is not to your liking, it is polite to at least make some attempt to eat a small amount of it. Or at the very least, cut it up a little, and move it around the plate.

6. It is quite acceptable to leave some food to one side of your plate if you feel as though you have eaten enough. On the other hand, don't attempt to leave your plate so clean that it looks as though you haven't eaten for days!

7. Desserts may be eaten with both a spoon and fork, or alternatively a fork alone if it is a cake or pastry style sweet.

8. Should a lady wish to be excused for the bathroom, it is polite for the gentlemen to stand up as she leaves the table, sit down again, and then stand once more when she returns.

9. Always make a point of thanking the host and hostess for their hospitality before leaving.

10. It is good dinner table etiquette to send a personal thank-you note to the host and hostess shortly afterwards.

Ⅳ. Listen and Talk

Sample:

Dinner Table Etiquette —The 10 Do's in China

1. Wait for the host to begin before you start eating or drinking. In Chinese etiquette the host always begins each dish by serving the guest of honor and one or two other guests nearby.

2. Sample at least a bite of every dish. Your host will be looking at you to see your fortitude.

3. Always offer food or tea to someone else before you serve yourself. You would be considered a pig and without manners if you serve yourself first.

4. Leave serving dishes on the table or lazy Susan rather than picking them up or passing them around. You may reach across others to get food from a serving dish.

5. Second helpings of foods are fine. However, cleaning your plate can mean the host did not provide enough food to satisfy you.

6. Do not take the last piece of food on the serving platter. It's considered bad luck, shows your greed, and seems you are too hungry to take the piece of a dish.

7. Give chopsticks a chance. Practice manipulating the world's oldest eating utensils (keep in mind that even little children use them in Asia). During a meal, it is considered rude and a sign of bad luck to lay your chopsticks vertically parallel on the top of the bowl or leave them sticking up in the bowl. Try not to drop your chopsticks either, as this, too, is a sign of bad luck. Most of all, in the absence of serving spoons, use the wider top end of your chopsticks, not the end that goes into your mouth, to take food from serving dishes.

8. Keep meal conversations light and general. Discuss the arts, food, and the well-being of children and family members during the meal, not business. As in all cultures, no politics or religion.

9. Avoid putting your hands in your mouth for any reason while at the table. If you must take something out of your mouth, such as bones, gristle, or another item, use your chopsticks and place the items to the side of your plate, or use a toothpick.

10. Use both hands to hold your glass when giving and receiving toasts. Customarily the host will begin the dinner with a toast of welcome. After the second or third course, the guest of honor might say a few words and return a toast. Chinese historically do not clink glasses. Lifting a glass with both hands to shoulder height shows the utmost respect.

Men and Women

Aims

- Listening to People Talking About Relationships
- Expressing Your Ideas

I Warm-up

Fill in the blanks with the following words.

households	spoil	confidence	person's	income
single-parent	spouse	childless	marriage	divorce

1. DINK families refer to families that have dual _____ and no kids.

2. The childless couple boom reflects the lack of _____ in their marriage in this ever-changing society.

3. One or two decades ago, there would be gossip around a married but _____ couple.

4. They don't want children to _____ their marriage.

5. Any couple who want a child should first be confident that their _____ is sound.

6. Due to the increasing divorce rate, there are more and more single-parent _____ .

7. Other results suggest that those who marry at a younger age are more likely to _____ .

8. Divorce usually causes a former _____ to move out and form a new household, thus increasing the size of materials and land for housing.

9. Divorce impacts on every single area of a _____ life.

10. Social scientists have found that children growing up in _____ families are disadvantaged in some ways when compared to those from two-biological-parent families.

Now listen and check.

LANGUAGE TIPS

gossip: 流言飞语；绯闻   spoil: 损害，损坏

spouse: 配偶   household: 一家人

sound: 可靠的

Ⅰ. Warm-up

 Scripts:

1. DINK families refer to families that have dual <u>income</u> and no kids.

2. The childless couple boom reflects the lack of <u>confidence</u> in their marriage in this ever-changing society.

3. One or two decades ago, there would be gossip around a married but <u>childless</u> couple.

4. They don't want children to <u>spoil</u> their marriage.

5. Any couple who want a child should first be confident that their <u>marriage</u> is sound.

6. Due to the increasing divorce rate, there are more and more single-parent <u>households</u>.

7. Other results suggest that those who marry at a younger age are more likely to <u>divorce</u>.

8. Divorce usually causes a former <u>spouse</u> to move out and form a new household, thus increasing the size of materials and land for housing.

9. Divorce impacts on every single area of a <u>person's</u> life.

10. Social scientists have found that children growing up in <u>single-parent</u> families are disadvantaged in some ways when compared to those from two-biological-parent families.

II Listening Focus: Describing Different Types of Families

Listen to the statements and fill in the blanks.

1. Since the 1960s, there has been a marked increase in the number of children living with a _____ .

2. Financial support is many times lost when an adult goes through a _____ .

3. Couples living in _____ households are thought to have more disposable income because they don't have the added expenses that come with children.

4. In 2000, _____ with the original biological parents constituted roughly 24.1% of American households.

5. It has often been presumed that _____ groups sharing a single household enjoy certain advantages, such as a greater sense of security and belonging due to sharing a wider pool of members to serve as resources during a crisis, and more role models to help perpetuate desired behavior and cultural values.

LANGUAGE TIPS

disposable: 用后即可丢弃的物品，一次性物品

constitute: 组成，构成

presume: 假定

perpetuate: 使永久

nuclear family: 核心家庭（只有父母和孩子的家庭）

extended family: 大家庭（含祖父母、父母和孩子的家庭）

II. Listening Focus: Describing Different Types of Families

> **TEACHING TIP**
>
> Families change with the development of economy. Explain different types of families to the students.

 Scripts:

1. Since the 1960s, there has been a marked increase in the number of children living with a single parent.

2. Financial support is many times lost when an adult goes through a divorce.

3. Couples living in DINK households are thought to have more disposable income because they don't have the added expenses that come with children.

4. In 2000, nuclear families with the original biological parents constituted roughly 24.1% of American households.

5. It has often been presumed that extended family groups sharing a single household enjoy certain advantages, such as a greater sense of security and belonging due to sharing a wider pool of members to serve as resources during a crisis, and more role models to help perpetuate desired behavior and cultural values.

 III Listening Practice

Task 1

Listen to the following passage, and choose the best answer to each of the questions.

1. What did the speaker notice one day?

   A. An old couple walked into McDonald's with difficulty.

   B. The old couple only ordered food enough for one person.

   C. An old man ordered meal for his wife only.

   D. An old woman ordered meal for her husband only.

2. Why did the speaker offer to buy another meal for the old couple?

   A. It was the speaker's responsibility to buy them another meal.

   B. The speaker thought they had had their wallet stolen.

   C. The speaker thought they were too poor to afford another meal.

   D. They are the speaker's old friends.

3. Why did the old man refuse the speaker's offer?

   A. He didn't want others to know they were poor.   B. He didn't like the food at McDonald's.

   C. His wife didn't like the speaker.   D. It was a habit for the old couple to share everything.

4. What could the speaker no longer stand?

   A. The old couple refused his offer again.

   B. The old man ate alone while the old woman only took a few sips of the drink.

   C. The old couple were angry about his offer.

   D. The old couple cheated him.

5. Why did the old woman eat nothing?

   A. She wanted to leave her food for her husband.   B. She had no appetite at McDonald's.

   C. They could not afford more food.   D. She waited for the artificial teeth.

III. Listening Practice

Task 1

TEACHING TIP

Play this part twice, and then ask the students to retell the story according to what they hear.

 Keys:

1. B   2. C   3. D   4. B   5. D

 Script:

I was having my dinner at McDonald's one evening when an old couple slowly walked in. They ordered their meal, took a table near the window and started taking food out of the plate. There was one hamburger, one order of French fries and one drink. The man divided the food into two halves and carefully placed one before his wife.

He took a sip of the drink. His wife also took one and then set the cup down between them. "That poor old couple! All they can afford is one meal for the two of them," thought I. As the man began to eat his French fries, I rose to my feet, went over and said that I was willing to buy another meal for them. But he kindly refused me and said that they made it a habit to share everything. Surprisingly, the lady didn't take a bite. She sat there watching her husband eat and taking turns sipping the drink. Again I asked to buy them something but was refused. When the man finished eating and was wiping his face with a napkin, I could no longer stand it. I made an offer to them the third time. After being politely refused, I asked the lady curiously, "Madam, why aren't you eating? You said you share everything. What is it that you are waiting for?" "The teeth," she answered.

Task 2

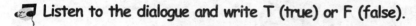 Listen to the dialogue and write T (true) or F (false).

_____ 1. Merry is going to have a baby.

_____ 2. DINK is the short term for "dual income, no kids."

_____ 3. Merry doesn't want children to involve in her life and spoil her marriage.

_____ 4. Having a baby will affect Nyssa's promotion in the company.

_____ 5. Merry doesn't want to have a baby to let her parents down.

LANGUAGE TIPS

mother-to-be: 准妈妈
romantic: 浪漫的
promotion: 晋升
let...down: 使失望，辜负

Task 2

 Keys:

1. F   2. T   3. F   4. F   5. F

 Script:

Merry: Congratulations, Nyssa. A mother-to-be!

Nyssa: Thanks. How about you, Merry? You've been married for several years.

Merry: I don't know yet. My husband and I have thought about it, but we're just not ready.

Nyssa: Do you want to be a DINK family?

Merry: What does that mean?

Nyssa: DINK is the short term for "dual income, no kids." It is said that young childless couples are a new trend in China.

Merry: Oh, really? I have no idea about that.

Nyssa: They choose so because they don't want children to involve in their life and spoil the marriage.

Merry: That's true. But we're not having kids right now for romantic reasons. We're just waiting for the right time.

Nyssa: Oh, I see. It takes time and energy to raise a child.

Merry: Definitely. You know I've just got a promotion in our company. If I have a baby now, I will miss a good opportunity.

Nyssa: I understand. I used to have the same problem as you.

Merry: I guess eventually I'll have one, as we don't want to let our parents down.

Nyssa: Good for you. Kids will bring you a lot of happiness.

Merry: Thank you.

Task 3: Listen for Fun

🎧 Listen to the story and answer the following questions in your own words.

1. What happened to the man and the woman?

2. What were the two miracles according to the woman?

3. What did the woman suggest when she found the bottle of wine?

4. Did the man take the woman's suggestion?

5. What would be the end of the story?

🎧 Listen to the story again and retell the story with the help of the answers to the questions.

LANGUAGE TIPS

demolish: 毁坏
reply: 回答，答复
celebrate: 庆祝，祝贺
swig: 大口地喝，痛饮

Task 3: Listen for Fun

 Keys:

1. They had a car accident and both of their cars were totally demolished.

2. One miracle was both the man and herself were not hurt, and another miracle was the bottle of wine did not break in the accident.

3. She suggested they drink the wine to celebrate their good fortune.

4. Yes, the man took a few large swigs.

5. The man was accused drunk driving.

 Script:

A woman and a man are involved in a car accident. Both of their cars are totally demolished but amazingly neither of them is hurt.

After they crawl out of their cars, the woman says, "Wow, just look at our cars! There's nothing left but fortunately we are not hurt. This must be a sign from God that we should meet and be really good friends."

The man thought there might be a bright side to this and replied, "I agree with you completely."

The woman continued, "And look at this, here's another miracle. My car is completely demolished but this bottle of wine didn't break. Surely we must drink this wine and celebrate our good fortune."

Then she hands the bottle to the man. The man nods his head in agreement, opens it and takes a few very large swigs from the bottle and then hands it back to the woman.

The woman takes the bottle, immediately puts the cap back on, and hands it back to the man. The man asks, "Aren't you having any?"

The woman replies, "No. I think I'll just wait for the police."

 **Look and Talk**

Men and Women—Equal at Last?

You are going to debate whether women are finally truly equal to men. Use the clues and ideas below to help you create an argument for your appointed point of view with your team members.

Model:

A: Women are now equal to men. You see, many governments have both male and female representatives nowadays. And many companies are now owned or managed by women.

B: Excuse me? Women still have a long way to go before they are equal to men. I think women still earn less than men in many work situations. And they are still portrayed in a superficial manner in many television shows.

LANGUAGE TIPS

equality: 平等
sexual harassment: 性骚扰
representative: 代表
portray: 描述

Now Your Turn.

Clues:

- Men now share in the raising of children and household responsibilities.
- Many important laws have been passed to ensure equality in the workplace.
- In many places, a married couple can choose whether the man or the women takes leave from work to look after the newly arrived baby.

- The vast majority of government workers are male.
- Women are often not given enough responsibility based on the possibility of pregnancy.
- The number of sexual harassment suits has increased over the past ten years.

IV. Look and Talk

 Sample:

I think men and women are equal today in China. You see many men share in the raising of children and household responsibilities.

I don't think so. Women today still take a main role in taking care of children and housework, not to mention women are often not given enough responsibilities based on the possibility of pregnancy.

Celebrities

Aims

- Listening to People Talking About Famous People
- Introducing a Person

I Warm-up

 Look at the pictures. Who are they? Please match the names and the pictures, and then briefly introduce them.

Martin Luther King	Michael Jackson	Steve Jobs
Michael Jordan	Liu Xiang	

A. _____

B. _____

C. _____

D. _____

E. _____

Ⅰ. Warm-up

 Keys:

A. <u>Michael Jackson</u>

B. <u>Steve Jobs</u>

C. <u>Michael Jordan</u>

D. <u>Martin Luther King</u>

E. <u>Liu Xiang</u>

Ⅱ Listening Focus: Talking About Famous People

Listen to the dialogue and mark the statements T (true) or F (false).

1. _____ There are four sports stars mentioned in this dialogue.

2. _____ There are four movie stars mentioned in this dialogue.

3. _____ In the eyes of Tom, movie stars are more famous than sports stars.

4. _____ Lucy thinks that sports stars work hard to achieve more for our country than movie stars.

5. _____ In 2009 Athens Olympic Games, Liu Xiang won the gold medal in 110 hurdle.

LANGUAGE TIPS

110 hurdle: 110 米跨栏

make great contribution to: 对……作出巨大贡献

II. Listening Focus: Talking About Famous People

> ## TEACHING TIP
>
> Ask the students to listen to the dialogue carefully and then mark the statements true or false. Then ask the students to retell the dialogue in their own words.

 ## Keys:

1. T   2. F   3. T   4. T   5. F

 ## Script:

Lucy: Hi, Tom. Do you know something about Liu Xiang?

Tom: Sure. Everyone knows about him. He is good at 110 hurdle, and is an excellent athlete in China.

Lucy: He won the gold medal in 2004 Athens Olympic Games, and then he became famous all over the world.

Tom: Do you think he is one of the famous people?

Lucy: Yes, I do. But there are many other famous sports stars in China, like Yao Ming, Guo Jingjing, Wang Hao and so on.

Tom: But I prefer movie stars, especially the ones from Hong Kong. I think they are more famous than sports stars.

Lucy: Then you like Zhou Xingchi, Zhou Runfa and Jackie Chan, don't you?

Tom: Yes, they are all famous stars with a lot of fans, including me. Do you like the movie stars?

Lucy: Frankly, I don't. I just like sports stars. I think they work hard to achieve more for our country.

Tom: Your words sound reasonable.

Lucy: And I like other famous persons from other countries too.

Tom: Who are they?

Lucy: They are Albert Einstein, Thomas Edison and they all made great contribution to human beings.

Tom: Yes, they are also famous ones we will never forget.

Lucy: In my opinion, famous people should be those who have great achievement for our society.

Tom: Uh, I agree with you.

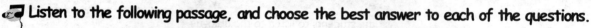

III Listening Practice

Task 1

🎧 Listen to the following passage, and choose the best answer to each of the questions.

1. Michael Jackson sold _____ albums over his career.

   A. 175 million   B. 750 million   C. 750 billion   D. 75 billion

2. Michael Jackson redefined popular culture with _____ .

   A. his energetic music   B. his dance moves   C. his revolutionary music videos   D. all the above

3. There are _____ children in Jackson's family in total.

   A. 5   B. 7   C. 9   D. 11

4. The album called _____ was not just the best-selling album and also won eight Grammy Awards and seven American Music Awards.

   A. *Off the Wall*   B. *Thriller*   C. *We Are the World*   D. *I Want You Back*

5. Which of the following statements is NOT true according to the passage?

   A. Michael Jackson was a huge success, but he was also a very troubled man.

   B. Michael Jackson left a huge mark on popular culture.

   C. Michael Jackson had many operations to change his face.

   D. Michael Jackson died of heart failure on June 25th, 2008.

LANGUAGE AND CULTURE TIPS

Michael Jackson: 迈克尔·杰克逊（1958.08.29—2009.06.25），被誉为流行音乐之王，是继猫王之后西方流行乐坛最具影响力的音乐家，其成就已超越猫王，是出色的音乐全才，在作词、作曲、场景制作、编曲、演唱、舞蹈、乐器演奏方面都有着卓越的成就。

King of Pop: 流行音乐之王   **album:** 唱片集   **energetic:** 精力充沛的；积极的；有力的

revolutionary: 革命的；大变革的   **release:** 发行，发布

Grammy Awards: 格莱美音乐大奖（美国国家录音与科学学会每年举行的一个年度大型音乐评奖活动）

Ⅲ. Listening Practice

Task 1

 Keys:

1. B   2. D   3. C   4. B   5. D

 Script:

Michael Jackson amazed the world with his music and dancing.

Michael Jackson, known as the "King of Pop," is one of the most famous performers in the world. Jackson sold more than 750 million albums over his career. He redefined popular culture with his energetic music, dance moves and revolutionary music videos.

Michael Jackson was born in Gary, Indiana in 1958. He was the seventh of nine children. He was five years old when he began singing with his brothers in a group called "The Jackson 5." Their first four songs were *I Want You Back*, *ABC*, *The Love You Save* and *I'll Be There*. They all reached the number one position in pop music record sales in 1970.

Three years later, Jackson released *Thriller*. The album was not just the best-selling album of all time, it also won eight Grammy Awards and seven American Music Awards.

Michael Jackson was a huge success, but he was also a very troubled man. He had many operations to change his face.

Michael Jackson died of heart failure on June 25th, 2009. Millions of his fans around the world mourned his death. However, Michael Jackson left a huge mark on popular culture. His memory will live on in his unforgettable music.

Task 2

📻 **Listen to the dialogue and mark T (true) or F (false) for each statement.**

1. _____ He Kexin had a perfect performance and she won the balanced beam.

2. _____ He Kexin performed so wonderfully that all the audience stood up.

3. _____ He Kexin has quite good skills in uneven bars.

4. _____ Yang Wei won the all-round champion.

5. _____ Yang Wei attributes his success to the help of his coach.

LANGUAGE TIPS

gymnastics: 体操
graceful: 优雅的，优美的
swift: 迅速的，敏捷的

Task 2

 Keys:

1. F　　　2. T　　　3. T　　　4. T　　　5. F

 Script:

Bob: Did you watch the performance of gymnastics last night?

Jim: Of course. He Kexin won uneven bars and her performance was so perfect!

Bob: Her performance looked so relaxed and graceful.

Jim: She was quite an experienced gymnast!

Bob: Right. The movement was so wonderful that all the audience stood up.

Jim: Yeah. It needs quite good skills and physical strength to do that.

Bob: Yes. Her landing was also swift and sure. And in Men's all-round championship, Yang Wei won the gold medal.

Jim: Yes, let's listen to the interview of Yang Wei.

Reporter: I'd like to congratulate you on earning all-round champion!

Yang Wei: Thank you!

Reporter: At the moment can you tell us your feeling?

Yang Wei: Very excited and happy.

Reporter: What do you want to say best?

Yang Wei: Thank my coach, my parents, my close players, and all the friends who support me fully. Thank you very much!

Reporter: Your coach is very kind to you, isn't he?

Yang Wei: Yes, and very strict with me. He was quite strict in every movement during the training; sometimes it seemed to be a little severe.

Reporter: I think it is very helpful to you.

Yang Wei: Now I understand it completely. I'm so grateful.

Reporter: Thank you for your time. Best wishes for you!

Task 3: Listen for Fun

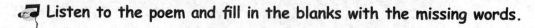 **Listen to the poem and fill in the blanks with the missing words.**

I Need You Now

My friend, I need you now —

Please _____ me by the hand.

Stand by me in my hour of _____ ,

Take time to _____ .

Take my hand, dear friend,

And _____ me from this place.

_____ away my doubts and fears,

Wipe the _____ off my face.

Friend, I cannot stand _____ .

I need your hand to hold.

The _____ of your gentle touch,

In my world that's _____ so cold.

Please be a friend to me,

And _____ me day by day.

Because with your loving hand in mine,

I know we'll find the way.

Task 3: Listen for Fun

 *Script:*

I Need You Now

My friend, I need you now—
Please <u>take</u> me by the hand.
Stand by me in my hour of <u>need</u>,
Take time to <u>understand</u>.

Take my hand, dear friend,
And <u>lead</u> me from this place.
<u>Chase</u> away my doubts and fears,
Wipe the <u>tears</u> off my face.

Friend, I cannot stand <u>alone</u>.
I need your hand to hold.
The <u>warmth</u> of your gentle touch,
In my world that's <u>grown</u> so cold.

Please be a friend to me,
And <u>hold</u> me day by day.
Because with your loving hand in mine,
I know we'll find the way.

Look and Talk

Task 1

 Look at the pictures. Please match the pictures with the names in the table and try your best to introduce them.

1. _____

2. _____

3. _____

4. _____

5. _____

6. _____

A. Yao Ming	B. Jackie Chan
C. Barack Hussein Obama	D. Kobe Bean Bryant Cocks
E. David Robert Joseph Beckham	F. Lady Gaga

Task 1

 Keys:

1. C   2. F   3. E   4. D   5. A   6. B

Task 2

 Create a dialogue with a partner for the following situation. Role-play the dialogue in front of the class.

 Sample

You and your partner are talking about the basketball stars.

A: NBA games have lost its relish in recent years, if only Michael Jordan had not retired!

B: I don't agree with you. As I see it, Kobe has carried on the value of Jordan.

A: So you like Kobe? They should not be mentioned in the same breath!

B: Different views. And I also appreciate Yao Ming, who was elected as one of the most influential sportsmen at the awards ceremony of the 60th anniversary for sports in China.

A: Yeah, I agree with you. He is the most influential player in the world sports. He lets us know more about NBA.

B: Yao Ming also throws himself into charity work and public service besides basketball and becomes the most famous sports celebrity.

A: Yeah, he is well deserved.

> ### LANGUAGE TIPS
>
> influential: 有影响力的
> throw oneself into: 积极从事，投身于
> charity: 慈善

Now Your Turn:

1. Work in pairs. Try to make a dialogue with the following situation.
2. Try to use the expressions listed below.

Useful Expressions: Talking About Titanic

Both you and your classmate are fans of James Cameron. You both like the movie *Titanic*, and now you are enjoying it in the cinema.

How do you like the director of *Titanic*, James Cameron?
How do you like the performance of Jack (Leonardo DiCaprio) and Rose (Kate Winslet) in the movie?
Do you believe that true love exists in the world?
In your opinion, what is true love?
How do you like the ending?

Task 2

 Sample:

A: Hi Mike, any plan for tonight?

B: Not really. It's raining; it's pouring. And everything is so boring.

A: Why don't you join me to watch the movie *Titanic*?

B: Is it an old movie?

A: Well, you may say that. It was released in 1997. I have seen it for a couple of times. But the more I see it, the better I like it.

B: What's so good about the movie? I saw it once. I know it was directed by James Cameron and starred by Leonardo DiCaprio and Kate Winslet. I like the movies from Cameron; he is an intelligent director.

A: Yeah, he definitely is. And Leonardo and Kate also well performed in the movie. They showed what is true love by their performance very vividly.

B: Yeah, in my opinion, true love should exist in our life.

A: Yes. There are quite a lot of memorable lines. That is why the movie remains so popular.

B: Are there any other reasons why you like the movie so much?

A: Of course. One thing I learn from the ending is true love is eternal.

B: Right. I agree with you. Let's cherish the one who loves us.

Enjoying Movies

Aims

- Listening to People Talking About Movies
- Making Comments

I Warm-up

 Fill in the blanks with the proper form of the following words and phrases.

LANGUAGE TIPS

window-shopping: 浏览商店橱窗
Academy Award/Oscar: 学院奖（奥斯卡金像奖）
box office: 票房
premier: 首次上映，首映
video: 视频，录像
contemporary: 当代的
blockbuster: 大片
be set in: 以……为背景

| Academy Awards | blockbuster | romance | contemporary movies | action films |
| box office | premier | video | be set in | be about |

1. For me it is quite something to sit watching the _____ directed by the world famous directors.

2. Compared with classic movies, I like _____ better.

3. *The Artist* which got five _____ is a black-and-white film.

4. _____ made by Jackie Chan won many children's heart.

5. *The Flowers of War* made by Zhang Yimou _____ 1937, Nanjing in China at the time of Sino-Japanese War.

6. *I Am Legend* _____ a man who survived a disaster in which a deadly virus has killed every healthy human on the island.

7. Since the late 1980s, Chinese films have enjoyed considerable _____ success abroad.

8. Henry is looking forward to the _____ of the new film.

9. Which do you like best among the different kinds of movies, such as comedy, _____ and science fiction?

10. Susan likes to watch _____ at home instead of going to the cinema.

Now listen and check.

Ⅰ. Warm-up

 Scripts:

1. For me it is quite something to sit watching the <u>blockbuster</u> directed by the world famous directors.

2. Compared with classic movies, I like <u>contemporary movies</u> better.

3. *The Artist* which got five <u>Academy Awards</u> is a black-and-white film.

4. <u>Action films</u> made by Jackie Chan won many children's heart.

5. *The Flowers of War* made by Zhang Yimou <u>is set in</u> 1937, Nanjing in China at the time of Sino-Japanese War.

6. *I Am Legend* <u>is about</u> a man who survived a disaster in which a deadly virus has killed every healthy human on the island.

7. Since the late 1980s, Chinese films have enjoyed considerable <u>box office</u> success abroad.

8. Henry is looking forward to the <u>premier</u> of the new film.

9. Which do you like best among the different kinds of movies, such as comedy, <u>romance</u> and science fiction?

10. Susan likes to watch <u>videos</u> at home instead of going to the cinema.

II Listening Focus: Terms Concerning Movies

Listen to the dialogues and fill in the blanks.

1. W: The movie was fantastic. Don't you think so?

   M: Yeah, the _____ was so good that you knew exactly what was going on. I laughed and cried during this movie, understood the _____ and related to them. A great, great movie!

   W: If movies were like this, I'd go every Saturday.

2. W: It is said Tom Hanks is going to _____ the movie.

   M: Really? You know I am a huge fan of Tom Hanks. Do you know who will _____ it?

   W: The famous director William Powell.

   M: Oh, my God, I love it. I love his movie's costume so much.

3. W: What do you think of the movie?

   M: I think the _____ was great, especially the _____ ; he is not just telling the story of Derek; he is telling the story of anyone and everyone who has felt the loss of their livelihood and identity as technology leaves them behind.

   W: I couldn't agree more.

4. W: Besides the first-class _____ , I think the _____ of the movie is cool.

   M: Well, don't you know it isn't hip any more?

   W: It is a classic. I can never like it enough.

5. W: The movie was boring. They didn't have many funny or meaningful _____ .

   M: Well, maybe. But I like the _____ of the movie. She is excellent.

   W: I doubt whether anyone can compare with her.

   M: But she alone still didn't save this film from becoming a bore of a story.

LANGUAGE TIPS

star: 由……主演，由……担任主角

costume: 服装，装束；戏装，剧装

cast: 演员阵容

line: 台词

heroine: 女主角

II. Listening Focus: Terms Concerning Movies

 Scripts:

1. W: The movie was fantastic. Don't you think so?

   M: Yeah, the <u>acting</u> was so good that you knew exactly what was going on. I laughed and cried during this movie, understood the <u>characters</u> and related to them. A great, great movie!

   W: If movies were like this, I'd go every Saturday.

2. W: It is said Tom Hanks is going to <u>star</u> the movie.

   M: Really? You know I am a huge fan of Tom Hanks. Do you know who will <u>direct</u> it?

   W: The famous director William Powell.

   M: Oh, my God, I love it. I love his movie's costume so much.

3. W: What do you think of the movie?

   M: I think the <u>casting</u> was great, especially the <u>hero</u>; he is not just telling the story of Derek; he is telling the story of anyone and everyone who has felt the loss of their livelihood and identity as technology leaves them behind.

   W: I couldn't agree more.

4. W: Besides the first-class <u>plot</u>, I think the <u>theme song</u> of the movie is cool.

   M: Well, don't you know it isn't hip any more?

   W: It is a classic. I can never like it enough.

5. W: The movie was boring. They didn't have many funny or meaningful <u>lines</u>.

   M: Well, maybe. But I like the <u>heroine</u> of the movie. She is excellent.

   W: I doubt whether anyone can compare with her.

   M: But she alone still didn't save this film from becoming a bore of a story.

III Listening Practice

Task 1

🎧 Listen to the dialogue and choose the best answer to each of the questions.

1. Who is Will Smith?

   A. He is an actor.   B. He is a man in black.

   C. He is Agent J.   D. He is a superman.

2. How difficult is it for Will Smith to play Agent J again?

   A. It is very difficult as it's been long since his last *MIB*.   B. It is not difficult at all like riding a bike.

   C. It is a little difficult like riding a black bike.   D. It is unbelievably difficult.

3. What era will Will Smith visit if he could travel back in time?

   A. The Tang dynasty.   B. India in the first century.

   C. Ancient Egypt.   D. Rome in the third century.

4. According to Will Smith, how do the "Women in Black" look?

   A. They are beautiful.   B. They are cold.

   C. They are frightening.   D. They are gentle.

5. Does Will Smith like *MIB* coming into 3D?

   A. Yes, he does.   B. No, he doesn't.

   C. Not mentioned.   D. Perhaps.

LANGUAGE AND CULTURE TIPS

MIB: Men in Black，《黑衣人》/《星际战警》

agent: 特工   *alien:* 外星人   *ancient:* 古代的

unique: 独特的   *cinematic:* 电影的，影片的

III. Listening Practice

Task 1

 Keys:

1. A   2. B   3. C   4. A   5. A

 Script:

Reporter: Will Smith, it's been quite a while since the last *MIB* and you have performed in a number of diverse films since. How difficult has it been getting back into the Agent J role after so long?

Will Smith: Not difficult at all! After you play a character twice, it's almost like riding a bike—a pretty black bike.

Reporter: Will, if you could travel back in time, which era would you visit and why?

Will Smith: Ancient Egypt—so I could prove that aliens didn't build the pyramids.

Reporter: Where are the "Women in Black"?

Will Smith: You gotta see the movie! There are some very prominent Women in Black, and they look hot, too.

Reporter: How do you feel about *MIB* coming out in 3D?

Will Smith: I just saw it in 3D—and it looks INSANE. It's the type of movie that is just supposed to be in 3D. Makes me want to go back and do the other two in 3D!

Reporter: What's your favorite part about being in the *MIB* movies?

Will Smith: I love that *Men in Black* is not like any other kind of movie. There's no other film I've ever seen that reminds me of *Men in Black*. *Men in Black* is very special and unique, and I think it will go down in cinematic history.

Task 2

🎧 Listen to the passage and choose the best answer for each question.

1. Who is threatening Po's new life?

A. The Dragon Warrior.   B. The Furious Five.

C. A villain.   D. Kung Fu.

2. How can Po stop the weapon?

A. He must look to his past and uncover the secrets of his mysterious origins.

B. He must look to his friend to uncover the secrets of his mysterious future.

C. He must look to his present and uncover the secrets of his mysterious present.

D. He must look to his future and uncover the secrets of his mysterious origins.

3. What is *Prom* about?

A. It is about a big dance.

B. It is about some relationships.

C. It is about the changeable path from high school to independence.

D. It is about love.

4. Why do the penguins seem terrible for Mr. Popper at first?

A. They make his life in order.   B. They turn his life upside down.

C. They give him a strange gift.   D. They make his work lousy.

5. What does Mr. Popper think of the penguins at last?

A. They are terrible.   B. They are a strange gift.

C. They are a curse.   D. They are a gift from God.

LANGUAGE AND CULTURE TIPS

threaten: 威胁到，危及

villain: 反派角色

conquer: 征服，克服，占领   origin: 血统，出身，来历

unfold: 逐渐显示，呈现   prom: 毕业舞会

inherit: 继承，成为继承人

turn...upside town: 搅得天翻地覆

TEACHING TIP

Play the recording three times, and then ask the students to talk with their partner about the films that they are looking forward to seeing and the reasons for it. Walk around the classroom and give help as needed.

Task 2

 Keys:

1. C   2. A   3. C   4. B   5. D

 Script:

Enjoy your life with movies. Here are plot summaries of three highly-recommended movies.

In *Kung Fu Panda 2*, Po's new life is threatened by the new villain, who plans to use an unstoppable secret weapon to conquer China and destroy Kung Fu. It is up to Po and the Furious Five to face this threat and defeat it. But how can Po stop the weapon that can stop Kung Fu? He must look to his past and uncover the secrets of his mysterious origins to stop the weapon.

At *Prom*, several intersecting stories unfold at one high school as the big dance approaches. *Prom* shows the changeable path from high school to independence as some relationships end and others begin.

In *Mr. Popper's Penguins*, Mr. Popper is a workaholic who is great at business and lousy at everything else. One day he inherits a very strange gift. Half of a dozen real-life penguins begin to turn his life upside down. At first they seem terrible, but soon Mr. Popper comes to see them as a gift from God.

Task 3: Listen for Fun

Listen to the song by the Candle Thieves and fill in the blanks with the missing words.

The Sunshine Song

I would buy you a _____
I would put it in the _____
If I _____ it down the river
Would you send it back to me?
I would pick you some flowers
I would put them where everyone could see
I would let the sun _____ on them
If you only smiled for me
'Coz you are beautiful but you've got to _____ someday
You know we can't _____ young forever
But we can stay young for the rest of our days
If you called me _____
Well I'm not sure what I would say
If you left me on your _____
Well I wouldn't go away
'Coz you are beautiful but you've got to die someday
And you are beautiful but you've got to die someday
You know we can't stay young forever
But we can stay young for the rest of our days
I would _____ up all your worries
I would put them in a _____ with all of mine
And I would find a way to make you happy
If I only had the time
You know we can't stay young forever
but we can stay young for the rest of our days
...

Task 3: Listen for Fun

 Script:

The Sunshine Song

I would buy you a <u>rainbow</u>

I would put it in the <u>stream</u>

If I <u>sailed</u> it down the river

Would you send it back to me?

I would pick you some flowers

I would put them where everyone could see

I would let the sun <u>shine</u> on them

If you only smiled for me

'Coz you are beautiful but you've got to <u>die</u> someday

You know we can't <u>stay</u> young forever

But we can stay young for the rest of our days

If you called me <u>indecisive</u>

Well I'm not sure what I would say

If you left me on your <u>doorstep</u>

Well I wouldn't go away

'Coz you are beautiful but you've got to die someday

And you are beautiful but you've got to die someday

You know we can't stay young forever

But we can stay young for the rest of our days

I would <u>pack</u> up all your worries

I would put them in a <u>jar</u> with all of mineAnd I would find a way to make you happy

If I only had the time

...

IV Look and Talk

 Look at the pictures. What did you think about the movies?

Model:

(*Mike and Susan are talking about the above movies.*)

M: What do you think about *Kung Fu Panda*?

S: Well, I think this cartoon is pretty good, but not as good as *The Adventures of TinTin*?

M: Really? But I think *Kung Fu Panda* is unbelievably good.

S: I think it is just OK. Why do you think so?

M: Well, the plot is first-class and I am impressed with the film's faithfulness to Chinese culture.

S: You're right. And there are many interesting and witty lines in the movie. But I still think *The Adventures of TinTin* is an excellent piece of work, especially the casting. It is so strong.

M: Yeah, *TinTin*'s really cool.

Now Your Turn:

1. Work in pairs to talk about the movies by using the given pictures.

2. Try to use other expressions listed below.

Useful Expressions: Making Comments

What did you think about…?   What's your opinion of…?
…is an excellent piece of work.   It's a/an wonderful/excellent/great movie.
…was incredible.   It's unbelievably good.
You can hardly imagine how wonderful the movie is.
One of the most amazing/impressive/striking things about the film is…
So many strange/beautiful/traditional/colorful costumes…
…the plot was first-class/superb.
…the character development was strong/good.
The acting was a little weak.   But the acting was not much good.
The casting was great.   The cast is strong.   They have all-star cast.
They just didn't have a lot of funny or meaningful lines.   They just didn't have many interesting and witty lines.
I can't imagine anyone else playing that part.   I don't think anyone can compete with him in playing/acting that part.
He's so cute.   He's sweet/lovable/adorable.

IV. Look and Talk

 Sample:

M: What did you think about the above films?

S: I think *The Dark Knight* is the best. I am crazy abut the superhero film.

M: Really? But I think *Roman Holiday* was unbelievably good. It is a movie worth watching many times, not only because of the attractive love story but also owing to the excellent performance of the leading actor and the leading actress. I don't think anyone can compete with them in playing/acting those parts. Audrey Hepburn gained the Academy Award for playing the leading female role in *Roman Holiday*.

S: Actually *The Dark Knight* received highly positive reviews and set numerous records. The film received eight Academy Award nominations and won two Academy Awards. *The Dark Knight* was so cool. I strongly recommend you to watch it.

M: Well, maybe I will, but I still love *Roman Holiday*. Each time I watched it, I laughed and cried, understood the characters and related to them. A great, great movie!

Environment

Aims

- Listening to People Talking About Environment Problems
- Working Out Solutions

 **Warm-up**

Fill in the blanks with the proper form of the following words and phrases.

environmental problems   effective measures   responsibility   severe   greenhouse gases
dry land   polluted   climate   deforestation   white pollution

1. We must take _____ to save our planet.

2. _____ is one of the greatest causes of global warming.

3. The _____ has been getting steadily warmer and warmer in recent years.

4. Water is _____ by waste from chemical factories.

5. Air pollution is a _____ problem which endangers our health.

6. Do you know that more than 70% of earth's _____ is affected by desertification?

7. _____ , the clearing of forests by cutting or burning trees, affects the life cycle of humans.

8. The pollution of plastic bags is also called _____ .

9. The Earth is facing many _____ , such as air pollution and water pollution and voice pollution.

10. Protecting the environment is not only the _____ of our government, but also our public.

Now listen and check.

LANGUAGE TIPS

greenhouse gas: 温室气体   climate: 气候
deforestation: 采伐森林   dry land: 旱地
desertification: 沙漠化   responsibility: 责任
white pollution: 白色污染

I . Warm-up

 Scripts:

1. We must take <u>effective measures</u> to save our planet.

2. <u>Greenhouse gases</u> is one of the greatest causes of global warming.

3. The <u>climate</u> has been getting steadily warmer and warmer in recent years.

4. Water is <u>polluted</u> by waste from chemical factories.

5. Air pollution is a <u>severe</u> problem which endangers our health.

6. Do you know that more than 70% of earth's <u>dry land</u> is affected by desertification?

7. <u>Deforestation</u>, the clearing of forests by cutting or burning trees, affects the life cycle of humans.

8. The pollution of plastic bags is also called <u>white pollution</u>.

9. The Earth is facing many <u>environmental problems</u>, such as air pollution, water pollution and voice pollution.

10. Protecting the environment is not only the <u>responsibility</u> of our government, but also our public.

II Listening Focus: How to Control Air Pollution

🎧 Listen to the dialogue and fill in the blanks.

A: The air in the city is seriously _____ .

B: Yes, I can't even breathe.

A: Air pollution _____ our health.

B: The government should take steps to _____ it.

A: How to control _____ pollution for the sake of people's health?

B: There are many methods _____ by the government. But it is pretty hard.

A: Why is that?

B: Some depurating devices are not so effective. Some effective devices are so _____ that manufacturers can't even afford.

A: Then why not consider reducing some _____ industries?

B: Almost impossible! China is a _____ country and needs heavy industries to increase its GDP.

A: Government should find out some effective measures as soon as possible to deal with air pollution.

B: Yes, you're right.

LANGUAGE TIPS

pollute: 污染   adopt: 采纳，采用   depurate: 净化，提纯

manufacturer: 制造商，制造厂   heavy industry: 重工业

GDP: gross domestic product 国内生产总值

II. Listening Focus: How to Control Air Pollution

 Script:

A: The air in the city is seriously <u>polluted</u>.

B: Yes, I can't even breathe.

A: Air pollution <u>endangers</u> our health.

B: The government should take steps to <u>solve</u> it.

A: How to control <u>air</u> pollution for the sake of people's health?

B: There are many methods <u>adopted</u> by the government. But it is pretty <u>hard</u>.

A: Why is that?

B: Some depurating devices are not so effective. Some effective devices are so <u>expensive</u> that manufacturers can't even afford.

A: Then why not consider reducing some <u>heavy</u> industries?

B: Almost impossible! China is a <u>developing</u> country and needs heavy industries to increase its GDP.

A: Government should find out some effective measures as soon as possible to deal with air pollution.

B: Yes, you're right.

 **Listening Practice**

Task 1

 Listen to the following passage, and choose the best answer to each of the questions.

1. Which is not mentioned in this passage?

   A. Cars have made the air unhealthy.   B. Factories have given off poisonous gases.

   C. People carefully disposed rubbish.   D. Waste water is continuously poured into rivers.

2. If the water is wasted and polluted, it will cause _____ .

   A. global shortage of sea water   B. global shortage of fresh water

   C. global shortage of salty water   D. global shortage of river water

3. According to the passage, global warming is caused by _____ .

   A. acid rain   B. ozone depletion

   C. over-exploitation of arable land   D. the rising density of carbon dioxide

4. Facing these environmental problems, some measures are being taken to solve them. Which is not

   mentioned in the passage?

   A. New laws must be passed to place strict control over industrial pollution.

   B. The public must receive education about environmental problems.

   C. The environmental problem is just the duty of the government.

   D. The government has taken actions to cope with these problems.

5. Which of the following statements is not true?

   A. Environmental problems are becoming very serious.

   B. Environmental problems are caused by natural changes.

   C. Pollution is threatening living species.

   D. A large quantity of resources are abused and wasted.

> **LANGUAGE TIPS**
>
> poisonous: 有毒的，有害的
> ozone depletion: 臭氧耗竭
> over-exploit:（对资源等的）过度开采
> carbon dioxide: 二氧化碳
> cope with: 处理

1. Write down some difficult new words on the board and ask the students to read and practice them.
2. Play this passage three times, and then ask the students to get the main idea of the whole passage and encourage them to answer the questions.

III. Listening Practice

Task 1

 Keys:

1. C   2. B   3. D   4. C   5. B

 Script:

Environment Problems

Environmental problems are becoming more and more serious all over the world. For example, cars have made the air unhealthy for people to breathe and poisonous gases are given off by factories. We can find that waste water is being poured continuously into rivers and rubbish is carelessly disposed everywhere. Pollution is, in fact, threatening our existence.

A large quantity of resources are abused and wasted, and then a series of problems appear as a result. For example, the water is wasted and polluted, that comes global shortage of fresh water; the air is polluted by the industrial waste gases, that comes acid rain and ozone depletion; the atmosphere was changed by the rising density of carbon dioxide, that comes globe warming; the forests and the arable land are over-exploited, that comes deforestation, desertification and the loss of living species.

The earth is our home and we have the duty to take care of it. We must face the situation and take actions to solve our environmental problems. Some measures have been taken to cope with these problems by the government; new laws must be passed to place strict control over industrial pollution; the public must receive the education about the environmental problems and so on.

We hope that all these measures will be effective and bring back a healthy environment.

Task 2

WORLD ENVIRONMENT DAY

5 JUNE

Forests: Nature at Your Service

In support of the UN International Year of Forests

UNEP

Listen to the following passage and write T (true) or F (false).

_____ 1. World Environment Day (WED) happens on June 5 every year.

_____ 2. WED was created by the United Nations General Assembly in 1973.

_____ 3. According to the passage, global warming is the most serious issue among today's environmental issues.

_____ 4. WED doesn't need to make people in poorer countries aware of the dangers to the environment.

_____ 5. WED helps raise worldwide awareness of the threats to our environment.

LANGUAGE AND CULTURE TIPS

World Environment Day (WED): 世界环境日

United Nations General Assembly：联合国大会。联合国6个主要机构之一，是唯一一个联合国所有成员国都参加的组织。联合国大会每年举行一次，也可召开特别会议。它主要是一个审议机构，可以对联合国宪章规定范围内的任何问题进行讨论并提出建议。大会主席每年从按地区划分的5个成员国集团中轮流选出。

tackle: 解决，处理   be aware of: 意识到，注意到，觉察到

consumption: 消耗，消费

TEACHING TIP

1. Explain "World Environmental Day (WED)" and give more information to the students.
2. Play this passage three times, and then ask the students to mark the statements true or false and then encourage the students to talk about their understanding about WED according to what they hear.

Task 2

 Keys:

1. T   2. F   3. T   4. F   5. T

 Script:

World Environment Day

World Environment Day (WED) is a day we all need to put in our diaries. It happens on June 5 every year and should be one of the most important days of the holiday calendar. WED was created in 1972 by the United Nations General Assembly. The environment wasn't such a big issue back then. It is one of the hottest topics in the world today. WED helps raise worldwide awareness of the threats to our environment. Many environmental agencies organize events based on different themes each year. These events encourage both governments and local communities to work together. This ensures environmental problems are tackled from a grass roots level and at a presidential level.

Many people in rich countries are aware of today's environmental issues. Even though many of the world's citizens know the issues, too few people do enough to combat them. Perhaps the most serious issue is global warming. WED could be the day to start changing our lifestyle forever to reduce our carbon footprint. Most of us use far too much energy. With a little thought, we could all use less power and help the environment. WED also needs to make people in poorer countries aware of the dangers to the environment. The governments of new emerging countries such as China and India need to reduce their energy consumption too. Hopefully, World Environment Day will become more celebrated every year.

Task 3: Listen for Fun

Listen to the song and fill in the blanks with the missing words.

Heal the World

There's a place in your _____

And I know that it is love

And this place could be brighter than tomorrow

And if you really _____

You'll find there's no need to cry

In this place you'll feel

There's no _____ or sorrow

There are ways to get there

If you _____ enough for the living

Make a little space

Make a better place

_____ the world

Make it a better place

For you and for me and the entire _____ race

There are people dying

If you care enough for the living

Make a better place for you and for me

If you want to know why

There's a _____ that cannot lie

Love is strong

It only cares for joyful giving

If we try

We shall see

In this bliss

We cannot feel _____ or dread

We stop existing

And start living

Then it feels that always

Love's enough for us growing

Make a better world

Make a better world

Heal the world

Make it a better place

For you and for me and the entire human race

...

Task 3: Listen for Fun

Heal the World

There's a place in your <u>heart</u>
And I know that it is love
And this place could be brighter than tomorrow
And if you really <u>try</u>
You'll find there's no need to cry
In this place you'll feel
There's no <u>hurt</u> or sorrow
There are ways to get there
If you <u>care</u> enough for the living
Make a little space
Make a better place
<u>Heal</u> the world
Make it a better place
For you and for me and the entire <u>human</u> race
There are people dying
If you care enough for the living
Make a better place for you and for me
If you want to know why
There's a <u>love</u> that cannot lie
Love is strong
It only cares for joyful giving
If we try
We shall see
In this bliss
We cannot feel <u>fear</u> or dread
We stop existing
And start living
Then it feels that always
Love's enough for us growing
Make a better world
Make a better world
Heal the world
Make it a better place
For you and for me and the entire human race

...

Ⅳ Look and Talk

 Look at the pictures. Please match the pictures with the sentences in the following table.

Picture 1 _____

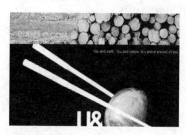

Picture 2 _____

Picture 3 _____

Picture 4 _____

Picture 5 _____

Picture 6 _____

1. If you waste plastic bags anymore, they will come back to harm you.
2. Have you thought that exhaust gases are polluting the air when you are comfortably driving?
3. Do you know the harmfulness of using disposable chopsticks?
4. Polluted water is a great danger to people's health. We hope there is no rubbish in the river.
5. How to protect our environment and create a green earth?
6. Global warming and ice melting are becoming a great threat to our environment.

LANGUAGE TIPS

plastic bag: 塑料袋

disposable chopsticks: 一次性筷子

exhaust gases: 废气

global warming: 全球气候变暖

ice melting: 冰雪融化

Model: (Picture 4)

A: Do you know that this winter will be another warm winter in the recent ten years?

B: Sure. Global warming is becoming more and more serious. They say in a few years maybe the Maldives will sink below the sea level.

A: What a shame! Maldives is such a beautiful place! I have dreamed of going there for a trip.

B: Besides, the ice of the North Pole begins melting, too. It's time we did something to prevent the trend; otherwise, pole bears will be homeless soon.

A: Exactly. With the development of modern technology, we enjoy a more convenient life while the harm we do to the environment is non-repairable. We burn fossil fuel and the emission of carbon dioxide is responsible for global warming.

B: Well, the increase in private cars also plays a part in it. So, what do you think we can do to help with environment protection?

A: To reduce the emission of greenhouse gas, we should try to find clean energy instead of contaminative coal or the like. And a limitation should be set for the consumption of conventional fuel and cars.

B: Yeah, it's still a long way ahead. We should call for the whole nation to do our best to protect our homeland — the earth.

Now Your Turn:

1. Work in pairs to make similar dialogues by using the given pictures.
2. Try to use other sentences and expressions listed below.

Useful Sentences and Expressions:

Global climate change is caused by…
Avoid using disposable chopsticks can save a forest.
White pollution refers to plastic pollution. Plastic shopping bags…
How to slow down global warming?
To get rid of … some effective measures should be taken to …
To prevent this nightmare from coming true, we should work together…

IV. Look and Talk

 Keys:

Picture 1 Have you thought that exhaust gases are polluting the air when you are comfortably driving?

Picture 2 Do you know the harmfulness of using disposable chopsticks?

Picture 3 Polluted water is a great danger to people's health. We hope there is no rubbish in the sea.

Picture 4 Global warming and ice melting are becoming a great threat to our environment.

Picture 5 If you waste plastic bags anymore, they will come back to harm you.

Picture 6 How to protect our environment and create a green earth?

 Sample:

Bonny and her group members are discussing their research work on pollution.

Bonny: We are going to do some research on the pollution of the Pearl River. Do you have any idea about it?

Jason: Since pollution is one of the biggest problems in the world, I'm sure a lot of people are interested in this topic.

Sarah: Polluted water is a great danger to people's health, so I think our work is very meaningful.

Bonny: And we can visit some factories along the river.

Jason: Good idea, because factories always pollute the environment by pouring waste water directly into rivers.

Bonny: We can also borrow some books on this topic.

Jason and Sarah: OK. Let's go to the library now.

Men and Animals

Aims

- Listening to People Talking About Animals
- Expressing Agreement or Disagreement

I Warm-up

LOOK! Fill in the blanks with the proper form of the following words.

reportedly	exotic	companion	bacteria	cute
garbage	playful	allergy	non-traditional	cooperative

1. A pet is a _____ as well as a responsibility.

2. Most _____ pets pose a risk to the health of young children.

3. Believe it or not, I found my cat by a _____ can around my neighborhood two years ago.

4. There are even rodents and monkeys! It's a world of _____ pets.

5. Most reptiles carry some harmful _____. They are likely to cause immune system problems.

6. I've always wanted a Springer Spaniel. She's so _____.

7. Zoo keepers have _____ trained a sea lion to write in Chinese.

8. Amazingly, the elephant was totally _____ during the two-and-a-half-hour operation.

9. Many animals are gentle, _____ and fun.

10. Some people have _____ to animals.

Now listen and check.

LANGUAGE TIPS

exotic: 奇异的，古怪的

allergy: 过敏

rodent: 啮齿动物（如老鼠、兔子等）

Springer Spaniel: 史宾格猎犬

reptile: 爬行动物

immune system: 免疫系统

Ⅰ. Warm-up

 Scripts:

1. A pet is a <u>companion</u> as well as a responsibility.

2. Most <u>non-traditional</u> pets pose a risk to the health of young children.

3. Believe it or not, I found my cat by a <u>garbage</u> can around my neighborhood two years ago.

4. There are even rodents and monkeys! It's a world of <u>exotic</u> pets.

5. Most reptiles carry some harmful <u>bacteria</u>. They are likely to cause immune system problems.

6. I've always wanted a Springer Spaniel. She's so <u>cute</u>.

7. Zoo keepers have <u>reportedly</u> trained a sea lion to write in Chinese.

8. Amazingly, the elephant was totally <u>cooperative</u> during the two-and-a-half-hour operation.

9. Many animals are gentle, <u>playful</u> and fun.

10. Some people have <u>allergies</u> to animals.

II Listening Focus

Listen for the specific words used to describe different animals.

1. Polar bears prefer eating _____ in the icy cold Arctic.

2. The population of elephants is _____.

3. Millions of sharks are killed for _____ each year.

4. Horses originally inhabit the desert and grasslands of _____ and Africa.

5. The wolf preys on all the large mammals in the _____.

LANGUAGE TIPS

brutal: 凶残的，残忍的
bleed: 流血
mammal: 哺乳动物
prey: 捕食

II. Listening Focus

 Keys:

1. Polar bears prefer eating <u>seals</u> in the icy cold Arctic.

2. The population of elephant is <u>decreasing</u>.

3. Millions of sharks are killed for <u>fin</u> each year.

4. Horses originally inhabit the desert and grasslands of <u>Asia</u> and Africa.

5. The wolf preys on all the large mammals in the <u>Northern Hemisphere</u>.

> **TEACHING TIP**
>
> Listen to the introduction to these animals twice and fill the blanks with the specific information.

 Scripts:

1. Polar bears live along shores and on sea ice in the icy cold Arctic. When sea ice forms over the ocean in cold weather, many polar bears, except pregnant females, head out onto the ice to hunt seals. When the warm weather causes the sea ice to melt, polar bears move back toward shore. Polar bears primarily eat seals.

2. At the turn of the 20th century, there were a few million African elephants and about 100,000 Asian elephants. Today, there are an estimated 450,000—700,000 African elephants and 35,000—40,000 wild Asian elephants. The population of elephants is decreasing greatly.

3. Today sharks are disappearing at an alarming rate. It is estimated that up to 75 million sharks are killed each year by "finning" alone. Shark finning is a brutal practice that involves cutting off a shark's fins, usually while it is still alive, and throwing the body back overboard where it either bleeds to death or drowns.

4. Horses are beautiful, graceful mammals that have long slender legs, a stocky body, and a long, narrow head. They are swift runners. They inhabit the desert and grasslands of Asia and Africa but have been introduced to many areas around the globe.

5. Wolf is truly a special animal. As the most widely distributed of all land mammals, the wolf is also one of the most adaptable. It inhabits all the vegetation types of the Northern Hemisphere and preys on all the large mammals living there.

III Listening Practice

Task 1

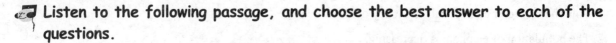

Listen to the following passage, and choose the best answer to each of the questions.

1. Why were the crops dying?

    A. The farm was destroyed by the strong wind.   B. There was no rain for almost a month.

    C. A flood had swept the field a month before.   D. The crops needed fertilizer badly.

2. How old was Billy?

    A. Eleven years old.   B. Five years old.

    C. Eight years old.   D. Nine years old.

3. Billy was giving water to _____ .

    A. a thirsty mother deer   B. a thirsty father deer

    C. a sick little deer   D. a lovely little deer

4. Billy was giving the deer water _____ .

    A. with a cup   B. with a bowl

    C. with a barrel   D. with his hands

> **LANGUAGE TIPS**
>
> amaze: 使惊讶
> exhaustion: 耗尽
> lap: 舔食，舔饮

5. Which of the following is true according to the story?

    A. The rain that came later that day saved their farm and the little boy saved a dying deer.

    B. The rain that came later that day saved their farm but the little boy didn't save the dying deer.

    C. The rain that came later that day didn't save their farm but the little boy saved a dying deer.

    D. The crops on the farm and the little deer died of lack of water.

Ⅲ. Listening Practice

Task 1

 Keys:

1. B   2. B   3. C   4. D   5. A

> **TEACHING TIP**
>
> Play the passage three times and ask the students to retell the story. Pay attention to the description of the details.

 Script:

It was one of the hottest days of the dry season. We had not seen rain for almost a month. The crops were dying at that time. If it didn't rain soon, we would lose everything. At noon, when I was in the kitchen making lunch, I saw my five-year-old son, Billy, walking towards the woods. Minutes later, he ran back and then once again walked towards the woods. This action—walking carefully to the woods and running back to the house, went on for nearly an hour. Finally I couldn't take it any longer and decided to follow him. As I entered the woods, I saw the most amazing sight. Two large deer appeared in front of him, and a little deer lying on the ground, clearly suffering from heat exhaustion, was lifting its head to lap the water cupped in my son's hands.

When the water was gone, Billy ran back to the house. I followed him back to the water tap. Billy turned it on and knelt over there, letting the drops slowly fill up the "cup" formed by his hands. When he stood up, I was there in front of him. His eyes just filled with tears. "I'm not wasting water, Mum," he said. "No, Billy, I am proud of you!" All I can say is the rain that came later that day saved our farm, just as one little boy saved a dying deer.

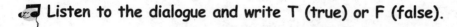

Task 2

🎧 Listen to the dialogue and write T (true) or F (false).

_____ 1. Mike is the man's new friend.

_____ 2. The woman doesn't want to have Mike because she is afraid that Mike will make her house messy.

_____ 3. The man plans to play frisbee with Mike in the future.

_____ 4. The man wants to feed meat and dog food to Mike.

_____ 5. The man thinks Mike will bring the house pleasure in the future.

LANGUAGE TIPS

security: 安全
burglar: 入室盗窃的夜贼
frisbee:（游戏用的）飞碟

Task 2

 Keys:

1. F   2. T   3. T   4. T   5. T

 Script:

Paul: Honey. Here is Mike. Do you like it?

Kate: What? You bring a dog into our house! It will mess up everything and shit everywhere. Don't let it enter the house! I've just swept the floor.

Paul: But honey, don't you think it's cute? It can give you a sense of security. Burglars will not dare to enter our house from now on.

Kate: No! It looks horrible. Look at its teeth! It's bearing its teeth to me!

Paul: Easy, easy, honey. It has noble blood—its father has won the championship of a worldwide dog show.

Kate: So are you sure it is tame? It won't bite me? It won't bark at us?

Paul: Yes, I'm sure. It will be a nice boy. This afternoon I'll take it out for a walk, and play frisbee with it. It'll love the game.

Kate: You have to feed it with meat, don't you?

Paul: Yes. We can also buy some dog food from the supermarket.

Kate: It will cost a lot of money.

Paul: Never mind. I'll work harder and earn more money. It will bring pleasure to our lives.

Task 3: Listen for Fun

Listen to the story and fill in the blanks with the missing words.

It was Monday, and Mrs. Smith's dog was very hungry, but there was not any meat in the house.

Considering that there was no better way, Mrs. Smith took _____ , and wrote: "Give my dog half a pound of meat." Then she gave the paper to her dog and said _____ , "Take this to the butcher, and he's going to give you your lunch today."

Holding the piece of paper in its mouth, the dog ran to _____ . It gave the paper to the butcher. The butcher read it carefully, recognized it was really the lady's handwriting and did as he was asked. The dog was very happy, and ate the meat up _____ .

At midday, the dog returned to the shop. It gave the butcher a piece of paper again. After reading it, he gave it half a _____ of meat once more.

The next day, the dog came again _____ at midday. And as usual, it brought a piece of paper in its mouth. This time, the butcher did not look at the paper, and gave the dog its meat, for he had _____ the dog as one of his customers.

But, the dog came again at four o'clock. And the same thing happened again. To the butcher's _____ surprise, it came for the third time at six o'clock, and brought with it a third piece of paper. The butcher felt a bit _____ . He said to himself, "This is a small dog. Why does Mrs. Smith give it so much meat to eat today?"

Looking at the piece of paper, he found that there were _____ words on it!

LANGUAGE TIPS

butcher: 屠户，肉贩

puzzle: 迷惑

TEACHING TIP

Listen to the passage twice and fill the blanks with the specific information. Ask the students to tell an interesting story they have experienced with an animal if you have time.

Task 3: Listen for Fun

It was Monday, and Mrs. Smith's dog was very hungry, but there was not any meat in the house.

Considering that there was no better way, Mrs. Smith took a piece of paper, and wrote: "Give my dog half a pound of meat." Then she gave the paper to her dog and said gently, "Take this to the butcher, and he's going to give you your lunch today."

Holding the piece of paper in its mouth, the dog ran to the butcher's. It gave the paper to the butcher. The butcher read it carefully, recognized it was really the lady's handwriting and did as he was asked. The dog was very happy, and ate the meat up immediately.

At midday, the dog returned to the shop. It gave the butcher a piece of paper again. After reading it, he gave it half a pound of meat once more.

The next day, the dog came again exactly at midday. And as usual, it brought a piece of paper in its mouth. This time, the butcher did not look at the paper, and gave the dog its meat, for he had regarded the dog as one of his customers.

But, the dog came again at four o'clock. And the same thing happened again. To the butcher's further surprise, it came for the third time at six o'clock, and brought with it a third piece of paper. The butcher felt a bit puzzled. He said to himself, "This is a small dog. Why does Mrs. Smith give it so much meat to eat today?"

Looking at the piece of paper, he found that there were not any words on it!

IV Listen and Talk

 Listen to the short story and share your understanding of the following two statements by combining what is mentioned in the story and what you have seen and heard in your own life.

1. The easiest way to lose love is to hold it too tight.

2. The best way to keep love is to give it wings.

Model:

I agree with the easiest way to lose love is to hold it too tight. The girl loved the first bird so deep that she was afraid of losing it and she held it tight. In the end, she killed the bird out of her love.

Now Your Turn.

IV. Listen and Talk

 Script:

Mary loved small animals very much. One morning while she was walking in the forest, she found two weak birds in the grass. She took them home and put them in a small cage. She cared them with love and the birds both grew strong. They thanked her with wonderful songs every morning.

But something happened one day. Mary left the door of the cage open. The larger bird flew from the cage. Mary thought it would fly away. As it flew close, she grasped it. She was very excited to catch it. Suddenly she felt strange. She opened her hand and looked sadly at the bird. Her great love had killed the bird! The other bird was moving up and forth in the cage. Mary could feel its great need for freedom. It wanted to fly into the clear and blue sky. At once, Mary took the bird out of the cage and let it fly away. The bird circled once, twice, three times…Mary enjoyed watching the bird flying and singing happily. Suddenly the bird flew closer and landed softly on her head. It sang the sweetest song that she had ever heard.

 Sample:

I agree with the second statement—the best way to keep love is to give it wings. After killing the first bird out of love, Mary set the second bird free. Seeing the bird flying freely in the clean blue sky and enjoying the sweetest song of the bird is one of the best ways to remain love.

图书在版编目（CIP）数据

基础实用英语听说教程（第三册）教师用书 / 崔振华主编. —北京：中国人民大学出版社，2012.12
新视界大学英语系列教材
ISBN 978-7-300-16854-8

Ⅰ.①基… Ⅱ.①崔… Ⅲ.①英语–听说教学–高等学校–教学参考资料 Ⅳ.①H319.9

中国版本图书馆 CIP 数据核字（2012）第 319871 号

新视界大学英语系列教材

基础实用英语听说教程（第三册）教师用书

总主编 马占祥
主 编 崔振华
副主编 林 涌
编 委 杨艳萍 刘 泉 李 慧 苏布德
　　　 王 倩 陈 焱 李晓英 胡啸翀

Jichu Shiyong Yingyu Tingshuo Jiaocheng (Di-san Ce) Jiaoshi Yongshu

出版发行	中国人民大学出版社	
社　　址	北京中关村大街31号	**邮政编码**　100080
电　　话	010–62511242（总编室）	010–62511398（质管部）
	010–82501766（邮购部）	010–62514148（门市部）
	010–62515195（发行公司）	010–62515275（盗版举报）
网　　址	http:// www.crup.com.cn	
	http:// www.ttrnet.com（人大教研网）	
经　　销	新华书店	
印　　刷	北京市易丰印刷有限责任公司	
规　　格	200 mm × 252 mm　16开本	**版　　次**　2013 年 1 月第 1 版
印　　张	7.75	**印　　次**　2013 年 1 月第 1 次印刷
字　　数	181 000	**定　　价**　21.00 元

中国人民大学出版社外语出版分社读者信息反馈表

尊敬的读者：

感谢您购买和使用中国人民大学出版社外语出版分社的 ＿＿＿＿＿＿＿ 一书，我们希望通过这张小小的反馈卡来获得您更多的建议和意见，以改进我们的工作，加强我们双方的沟通和联系。我们期待着能为更多的读者提供更多的好书。

请您填妥下表后，寄回或传真回复我们，对您的支持我们不胜感激！

1. 您是从何种途径得知本书的：
   □书店　　　　□网上　　　　□报纸杂志　　　　□朋友推荐
2. 您为什么决定购买本书：
   □工作需要　　□学习参考　　□对本书主题感兴趣　　□随便翻翻
3. 您对本书内容的评价是：
   □很好　　　　□好　　　　□一般　　　　□差　　　　□很差
4. 您在阅读本书的过程中有没有发现明显的专业及编校错误，如果有，它们是：

   ＿＿＿＿＿＿＿＿＿＿＿＿＿＿＿＿＿＿＿＿＿＿＿＿＿＿＿＿＿＿＿＿

   ＿＿＿＿＿＿＿＿＿＿＿＿＿＿＿＿＿＿＿＿＿＿＿＿＿＿＿＿＿＿＿＿

5. 您对哪些专业的图书信息比较感兴趣：

   ＿＿＿＿＿＿＿＿＿＿＿＿＿＿＿＿＿＿＿＿＿＿＿＿＿＿＿＿＿＿＿＿

   ＿＿＿＿＿＿＿＿＿＿＿＿＿＿＿＿＿＿＿＿＿＿＿＿＿＿＿＿＿＿＿＿

   ＿＿＿＿＿＿＿＿＿＿＿＿＿＿＿＿＿＿＿＿＿＿＿＿＿＿＿＿＿＿＿＿

6. 如果方便，请提供您的个人信息，以便于我们和您联系（您的个人资料我们将严格保密）：
   您供职的单位：＿＿＿＿＿＿＿＿＿＿＿＿＿＿＿＿＿＿＿＿＿＿＿
   您教授的课程（教师填写）：＿＿＿＿＿＿＿＿＿＿＿＿＿＿＿＿＿
   您的通信地址：＿＿＿＿＿＿＿＿＿＿＿＿＿＿＿＿＿＿＿＿＿＿＿
   您的电子邮箱：＿＿＿＿＿＿＿＿＿＿＿＿＿＿＿＿＿＿＿＿＿＿＿

请联系我们：鞠方安　商希建　黄婷　程子殊　于真妮

电话：010-62515576，62514974，62512737，62513265，62515037

传真：010-62514961

E-mail：jufa@crup.com.cn　　shandysxj@163.com　　huangt@crup.com.cn

　　　　chengzsh@crup.com.cn　　yuzn@crup.com.cn

通讯地址：北京市海淀区中关村大街甲 59 号文化大厦 15 层　　邮编：100872

中国人民大学出版社外语出版分社